AI or Die

The No-Nonsense SME / SMB
Guide to Getting Ahead in AI
(Before Your Competitors Do)

DARREN SMITH

Copyright © 2025 by Darren Smith

All rights reserved. This eBook, paperback or hardcopy book, or any portion thereof, may not be reproduced, distributed, or transmitted in any form or by any means, electronic or mechanical, including photocopying, recording, or by any information storage and retrieval system, without the prior written permission of the author, except for brief quotations in critical reviews and certain other non-commercial uses permitted by copyright law. This is a work of NON-FICTION. Names, characters, businesses, places, events, and incidents are either the products of the author's imagination or used in a fictitious manner. Any resemblance to actual persons, living or dead, or actual events is purely coincidental.

For permissions requests, please contact: smithsmerchant@gmail.com

Table of Contents

Forward 1

Part I – Foundations 3
Chapter 1 – AI Reality Check – Separating Signal from Noise 5
Chapter 2 – The SME Advantage – Why Smaller is Better for AI Implementation.... 15
Chapter 3 – AI Business Impact Framework 31

Part II – Strategic Planning 45
Chapter 4 – Your AI Readiness Assessment 47
Chapter 5 – The Four Pillars of AI Success: 55
Chapter 6 – Building Your AI Strategy Roadmap 67

Part III – Functional Applications 79
Chapter 7 – AI in Operations – Automating the Engine Room 81
Chapter 8 – Marketing and Sales AI – From Leads to Loyalty 95
Chapter 9 – HR and People AI 107

Part IV – Implementation 117
Chapter 10 – Getting Started 119
Chapter 11 – Data Foundations 131
Chapter 12 – Technology Choices – Build, Buy, or Partner: 141

Part V – Scaling And Optimisation 161
Chapter 13 – Scaling What Works 163
Chapter 14 – Managing AI Risks, Ethics, and Compliance – Don't Skip This One! . 175
Chapter 15 – Building an AI-Ready Culture 191

Part VI – Looking Forward 203
Chapter 16 – Measuring AI ROI 205
Chapter 17 – Future-Proofing Your Business 221
Chapter 18 – The AI Horizon for SMEs 233

FORWARD

Your primary competitive threat isn't the established firm across town; it's the AI-enabled startup that launched last month and is quickly capturing your customer base and market share. Whilst FTSE 100 companies invest millions in AI transformation initiatives, you may be questioning whether your small to mid-sized business can compete effectively in this landscape. The evidence is unequivocal: 73% of businesses that fail to adopt AI will become obsolete within five years, whilst 89% of SMEs that implement AI strategically will dominate their respective markets.

This is not another technical tome authored by Silicon Valley theorists who have never managed operational budgets or staff overheads. This is a comprehensive, practical guide for implementing AI solutions without compromising financial stability, overwhelming your workforce, or your company values. Whether you're a Chief Executive protecting your established market position, an Operations Director seeking competitive operational advantages, or a professional who has been tasked with AI implementation within a small budget and three months to prove AI has any value, this book will transform your perspective from AI apprehension to AI advantage.

The fundamental question is not whether AI will revolutionise your industry sector. The critical question is: will you be leading that transformation, or will you become its casualty?

This book is organised to clearly identify where and how AI can support your business, with very practical steps you can take right now. There are chapters on getting your business ready for success in AI; this is essential, and you in the SME sector have an advantage over larger businesses in this area. Moving through preparation, data, culture and implementing your first AI project. Key internal departments get their own section as well. You will find the structure includes representative case studies, pragmatic tips, a 'view' from the consultant and the actual tools, free through to paid for.

PART I
FOUNDATIONS

CHAPTER 1

AI Reality Check - Separating Signal from Noise

Understanding What AI Can and Cannot Do for Your Business Today

Artificial Intelligence (AI) is everywhere in the business conversation, promising to revolutionise everything from customer service to financial forecasting. Yet, for small and medium-sized enterprises (SMEs), the reality of AI is often clouded by hype, misconceptions, and uncertainty. This chapter provides a grounded, practical look at what AI can truly deliver for SMEs right now, what it can't, and how to cut through the noise to make smart, actionable decisions.

1. The State of AI for SMEs in 2025

AI has rapidly moved from the realm of tech giants to become an accessible, practical tool for businesses of all sizes. In 2025, over 80% of midsized companies investing in AI report operational cost reductions within their first year, often with solutions that are cheaper and easier to implement than most expect. For small businesses, AI is increasingly embedded in everyday tools, from accounting software to customer relationship management (CRM) platforms.

Key Takeaway:
AI is no longer reserved for enterprises with deep pockets or technical teams. Modern AI solutions are designed for business users, require minimal training, and are often bundled into the software SMEs already use.

AI's journey into the SME sector has been accelerated by a convergence of factors: the proliferation of cloud-based software, the rise of affordable subscription models, and the increasing integration of AI features into mainstream business tools. For example, accounting platforms like QuickBooks now offer AI-driven expense categorisation and fraud detection, while email marketing tools such as Mailchimp use AI to optimise send times and subject lines for better engagement.

For example, a small retailer using Shopify can now access built-in AI analytics to identify best-selling products, forecast inventory needs, and automatically segment customers for targeted promotions, all without hiring a data scientist or investing in custom software.

2. What AI Can Do for Your Business Today

a. Automate Repetitive Tasks

AI excels at automating routine, rules-based work; think invoice processing, appointment scheduling, and data entry. This frees up staff for higher-value, customer-facing, or creative tasks.

Beyond classic examples like invoice processing, SMEs can use AI-powered tools such as Zapier or n8n to connect different apps and automate multi-step workflows. For instance, when a new customer fills out a web form, an AI-enabled automation can create a CRM record, send a personalised welcome email, and schedule a follow-up call all without manual intervention.

Actionable Example:
A local cleaning company uses Tidio (an AI chatbot platform) to handle booking requests and answer FAQs on their website, reducing admin time by 10 hours per week.

b. Enhance Decision-Making

AI-powered analytics can process large volumes of business data, surfacing trends and insights that would be missed by manual analysis. For example, retailers use AI to forecast demand with up to 85% accuracy, optimising inventory and reducing stockouts.

AI isn't just for big data. Even modest datasets like monthly sales or website visits can be analysed by AI tools to spot patterns and recommend actions. Tools like Zoho Analytics or Microsoft Power BI now offer AI-driven insights that flag unusual trends or predict future sales.

Actionable Example:
A 12-person consultancy uses Power BI's "Quick Insights" feature to automatically surface which services are most profitable and which clients are at risk of churn, enabling smarter resource allocation.

c. Personalize Customer Interactions

AI-driven chatbots and recommendation engines deliver tailored experiences, boosting customer satisfaction and conversion rates. Many CRMs now suggest the best time to follow up with prospects or flag at-risk customers automatically.

AI chatbots (e.g., ChatGPT, ManyChat) can be trained on your business FAQs and tone of voice, delivering instant, consistent customer support even outside business hours. Recommendation engines, available in e-commerce platforms like Wix and Shopify, suggest products based on browsing and purchase history, increasing upsell opportunities.

Actionable Example:
A small online bookshop implements a recommendation widget that boosts average order value by 18% by suggesting relevant titles to shoppers.

d. Improve Financial Management

AI can automate invoice reminders, flag overdue payments, and even optimise cash flow, cutting down on the millions of hours SMEs spend chasing late payments each year.

AI-driven invoice automation platforms like Xero or QuickBooks can flag anomalies, send reminders, and even predict cash flow shortfalls. This helps SMEs avoid late payments and maintain healthier finances.

Actionable Example:
A construction subcontractor automates invoice follow-ups, reducing overdue payments from 25% to 8% in six months.

e. Support Scalability

AI-as-a-Service (AIaaS) and no-code/low-code platforms allow SMEs to scale AI solutions as they grow, without heavy upfront investment or technical expertise.

No-code AI platforms like Peltarion or MonkeyLearn allow SMEs to experiment with custom AI models such as sentiment analysis or document classification without hiring developers. As the business grows, these solutions can be scaled up or integrated with more advanced systems.

Actionable Example:
A marketing agency starts with a free AI sentiment analysis tool to monitor client brand mentions and then upgrades to a paid plan as their client base expands.

3. What AI Cannot (Yet) Do for SMEs

a. Replace Human Judgment and Creativity

AI is a tool, not a replacement for strategic thinking, empathy, or creative problem-solving. Gut feelings and experience still matter, especially in complex or ambiguous situations.

While AI can suggest which products to promote or which leads to prioritise, it cannot understand your business context, relationships, or strategic vision. For example, AI might recommend discounting a slow-moving product, but only a business owner knows if that product is essential for customer loyalty or brand positioning.

b. Work Without Good Data

AI's effectiveness depends on the quality and availability of your business data. Poor, incomplete, or siloed data limits what AI can achieve.

If your CRM is full of duplicate or outdated contacts, or your sales data is incomplete, AI's recommendations will be unreliable. Investing in data hygiene – regularly cleaning and updating records is a prerequisite for effective AI use.

Actionable Example:
Before adopting AI-driven marketing automation, a catering company spends a week cleaning its customer database, removing duplicates and updating contact info, ensuring that AI-powered campaigns reach the right audience.

c. Guarantee Instant ROI

While many SMEs see rapid efficiency gains, AI is not a "magic bullet. " Realising value requires clear goals, process alignment, and ongoing monitoring.

AI projects require clear objectives and realistic timelines. For example, a chatbot may need weeks of fine-tuning before it consistently handles customer queries without escalation.

d. Eliminate the Need for Change Management

AI adoption brings change. Staff may fear job loss or struggle to adapt to new workflows. Success depends on strong leadership, clear communication, and training, not just technology.

Staff buy-in is critical. Even the best AI tool will fail if employees don't trust or understand it. SMEs should plan for training sessions, open Q&A forums, and ongoing support as part of any AI rollout.

e. Solve Every Business Problem

Some challenges, like building a unique company culture or negotiating complex deals, remain squarely in the human domain.

AI can't replace personal relationships, negotiation skills, or the creative spark behind a new product idea. It's a complement, not a substitute, for human ingenuity.

4. Overcoming Common SME AI Myths

- Myth: "AI is too expensive or complex for us."
  Reality: Most modern AI tools are affordable, user-friendly, and require no coding. Many are embedded in the SaaS platforms you already use.

- Myth: "We need data scientists to use AI."
  Reality: Many AI features are now "invisible", working in the background of everyday apps and requiring little technical expertise.

- Myth: "AI will replace all our jobs."

Reality: AI typically augments human work, automating routine tasks so staff can focus on higher-value activities. Most SMEs report improved productivity and job satisfaction, not mass layoffs.

Practical AI Tools for SMEs (2025)

Function	Free/Low-Cost Option	Paid/Enterprise Option
Automation	Zapier Free, N8N Community	Zapier Pro, N8N Pro (£43/mo)
CRM & Sales	HubSpot Free, Zoho CRM	Salesforce Starter (£20+/mo)
Scheduling	Calendly Free	Calendly Pro (£8/user/mo)
Financial Management	Wave Free, QuickBooks	Xero, QuickBooks AI (£12/mo)
Customer Service	Tidio Free, ChatGPT Free	ChatGPT Plus (£16/mo), Drift

How to Get Started: A Pragmatic Approach

1. Identify a Pain Point: Start with a repetitive, time-consuming task or a clear business challenge.
2. Choose Accessible Tools: Look for AI features in platforms you already use, or trial free/low-cost options.
3. Set Clear Goals: Define what success looks like (e.g., hours saved, errors reduced, revenue increased).

4. Pilot and Measure: Test on a small scale, track results, and gather staff feedback.
5. Iterate and Scale: Expand what works, and stay informed about new AI features and best practices.

Real-World Case Studies (illustrative)

Case Study 1: Micro Business (Under 10 Staff)

Company: Fresh Grounds Coffee Shop (8 employees, UK)

Challenge:
The owner was overwhelmed by administrative tasks—managing bookings, tracking inventory, and responding to customer emails—leaving little time for customer engagement or business growth.

AI Solution:

- Calendly Free: Automated customer bookings and staff scheduling.
- QuickBooks AI: Automated invoicing and expense tracking, flagging late payments for follow-up.
- ChatGPT Plus (£16/mo): Draughted responses to common customer queries and managed online reviews.

Results:

- 8+ hours/week saved on admin.
- 30% reduction in missed appointments and double bookings.
- Customer response time improved from 24 hours to under 2 hours.
- Owner freed up to focus on customer experience and new menu launches.

Key Lesson:
Affordable, off-the-shelf AI tools can deliver immediate, measurable impact for even the smallest businesses without requiring technical expertise or major investment.

Case Study 2: Medium Enterprise (Under 200 Staff) (illustrative)

Company: Nova Retail Group (120 employees, UK)

Challenge:
Manual inventory management led to frequent stockouts and overstock, while customer service teams struggled to keep up with queries during peak periods.

AI Solution:

- Zoho CRM with Zia AI: Automated sales forecasting and customer segmentation, enabling smarter inventory planning and personalised marketing.
- Zapier Pro (£20/mo): Integrated e-commerce, CRM, and inventory systems, automating order processing and supplier notifications.
- Tidio AI Chatbot: Handled routine customer queries 24/7, freeing staff for complex cases.

Results:

- 20% reduction in inventory holding costs.
- 35% drop in customer service response times.
- Improved sales forecast accuracy, reducing both stockouts and excess inventory.
- Customer satisfaction scores increased by 18%.

Key Lesson:

Mid-sized SMEs can achieve enterprise-level efficiency and customer experience by integrating AI across core business functions—without the need for custom development or a large IT team.

Conclusion: Cutting Through the Hype

AI is real, practical, and ready for SMEs today—but it's not magic. The winners will be those who separate signal from noise, focusing on clear business value and pragmatic adoption. By starting small, leveraging user-friendly tools, and keeping people at the heart of the process, SMEs can unlock AI's power to save costs, delight customers, and drive sustainable growth.

CHAPTER 2

The SME Advantage - Why Smaller is Better for AI Implementation

How agility and focus give you the edge over enterprise competitors

There's a persistent myth in the business world that AI is only for tech giants and large corporations with deep pockets and armies of data scientists. I'm here to tell you that's not just wrong; it's backwards. After implementing AI solutions across hundreds of small and medium enterprises, I've discovered something that might surprise you: being smaller is actually your competitive advantage when it comes to AI implementation.

While Fortune 500 companies struggle with committee approvals, legacy system integration, and corporate bureaucracy, SMEs are quietly deploying AI solutions that deliver real business value in weeks, not years. Let me show you why your size isn't a limitation; it's your secret weapon.

In 2025, the AI landscape has shifted decisively in favour of SMEs. The myth that AI is only for tech giants is being dismantled by a new wave of affordable, plug-and-play solutions designed specifically for smaller businesses. According to SMEunited, SMEs are not just adopting AI; they are thriving, using it to automate, personalise, and make smarter decisions faster than ever before. The cost of entry has plummeted, with cloud-based platforms and SaaS tools offering AI capabilities for monthly fees that fit even the tightest budgets.

The Enterprise AI Paradox

Large corporations certainly have resources that SMEs don't have: bigger budgets, dedicated IT teams, and access to cutting-edge technology. But they also have something that often proves to be their Achilles' heel: complexity.

Illustrative example:
I recently worked with a global manufacturing company that spent 18 months and £2.3 million trying to implement a predictive maintenance system across their facilities. The project required approval from seven different departments, integration with twelve legacy systems, and compliance with corporate standards that hadn't been updated since 2018. By the time they launched, the original business problem had evolved, and the solution was already outdated.

Meanwhile, a 35-person engineering firm I advised implemented a similar predictive maintenance system in six weeks for £15,000. Their system is now preventing equipment failures, reducing downtime by 40%, and saving them approximately £180,000 annually.

The difference? Agility, focus, and the ability to make decisions quickly.

Why Now?

- The competitive gap is closing: SMEs that move quickly are capturing market share and building customer loyalty that late adopters will struggle to match.
- Customer expectations have evolved: people now expect instant, personalised, and seamless digital experiences, something AI delivers at scale.

- AI is a necessity, not a luxury: In payments, marketing, operations, and customer service, AI is now the foundation for efficiency, security, and growth.

Your Five SME Superpowers

Let me walk you through the specific advantages that give SMEs the edge in AI implementation:

1. Decision Speed and Authority

In most SMEs, the person who identifies a problem can often greenlight a solution within days. You don't need to navigate layers of management, committee approvals, or bureaucratic processes that can take months in larger organisations.

This speed advantage is crucial in AI because the technology landscape evolves rapidly. A solution that takes 18 months to approve and implement may be obsolete by the time it goes live. SMEs can spot an opportunity, test a solution, and scale it while larger competitors are still in the planning phase.

2. Laser-Focused Problem Solving

Large enterprises often try to solve multiple problems simultaneously, leading to complex, expensive solutions that satisfy no one completely. SMEs have the luxury of focusing on one specific pain point at a time.

This focused approach means you can:

- Clearly define success metrics
- Choose the right tool for the specific job
- Measure impact more accurately
- Iterate and improve quickly

3. Direct Stakeholder Involvement

In SMEs, the people who will use the AI solution are often directly involved in its selection and implementation. This eliminates the "telephone game" effect where requirements get distorted as they pass through multiple layers of management.

When the sales manager who struggles with lead qualification is directly involved in choosing and testing an AI lead scoring system, you get better requirements, faster buy-in, and more effective implementation.

4. Flexible Technology Stack

SMEs aren't burdened by decades of legacy systems that must be preserved at all costs. You can choose the best AI solution for your needs without worrying about compatibility with a mainframe system from 1987.

This flexibility allows you to:

- Adopt cloud-based AI services quickly
- Switch solutions if something isn't working
- Integrate new technologies with existing workflows
- Scale up or down based on actual needs

5. Cultural Adaptability

Smaller organisations typically have more nimble cultures that can adapt to new technologies faster. Change management is one of the biggest barriers to AI adoption in large companies and is often much simpler in SMEs.

The Art of Strategic Constraints

Here's something that might sound counterintuitive: having limited resources is actually an advantage when it comes to AI implementation.

Constraints force you to be strategic and creative in ways that unlimited budgets don't.

When you can't afford to hire a team of data scientists, you look for solutions that work out of the box. When you can't spend two years on a project, you focus on immediate value. When you can't integrate with every system, you choose the integration that matters most.

These constraints lead to better decisions, faster implementations, and more measurable results.

SME AI Success Patterns

After working with hundreds of SMEs, I've identified common patterns in successful AI implementations:

Start Small, Think Big: Successful SMEs begin with pilot projects that solve specific problems but choose solutions that can scale. They don't try to revolutionise their entire business overnight.

Embrace "Good Enough": While enterprises often get caught up in pursuing perfect solutions, successful SMEs implement AI that's good enough to deliver value, then improve it iteratively.

Focus on Business Outcomes: SME AI projects succeed when they have clear, measurable business goals rather than technology goals. The question isn't "How can we use AI?" But "How can we solve this specific business problem?"

Leverage Existing Relationships: SMEs often have closer relationships with customers and suppliers, making it easier to get feedback on AI implementations and adjust accordingly.

Pragmatic Actions for SMEs: Turning Advantage into Results

1. **Identify Quick-Win Use Cases:** Start with a single, high-impact area like automating customer support, streamlining payments, or optimising inventory. For example, many SMEs deploy AI chatbots (Tidio, ChatGPT, or ManyChat) on their websites to handle FAQs and booking requests, delivering 24/7 support without extra staff.

2. **Leverage Plug-and-Play AI Tools:** Choose off-the-shelf solutions that require no coding or technical expertise. Tools like Zoho CRM's Zia AI, QuickBooks AI, or Microsoft 365 Copilot offer AI-powered automation and analytics right out of the box. For marketing, Mailchimp's AI-driven campaign optimisation can increase open rates and conversions with minimal setup.

3. **Build Data Readiness:** Before launching any AI project, review your data quality. Clean up customer lists, sales records, and supplier databases. Good data is the fuel for effective AI, and even basic steps like de-duplicating contacts or standardising product names can make a big difference.

4. **Foster a Culture of Experimentation:** Encourage your team to try new tools and share feedback. SMEs that create "sandbox" environments where staff can safely test AI features—learn faster and adapt more quickly to change. Celebrate small wins and use them to build momentum for broader adoption.

5. **Collaborate with Experts and Peers:** Don't go it alone. Many SMEs benefit from working with AI consultants or joining peer networks to share best practices. Platforms like Tanhill.ai offer AI use case generators and readiness assessments tailored for SMEs, helping you prioritise and plan your AI journey.

6. **Prioritize Security and Compliance:** AI-powered security tools can help SMEs detect fraud and cyber threats in real time, protecting valuable data and customer trust. Choose vendors with strong compliance credentials and clear data handling policies.

7. **Measure and Iterate:** Set clear, business-focused metrics for every AI project, such as hours saved, error rates reduced, or sales increased. Use built-in dashboards or simple spreadsheets to track progress, and be ready to adjust quickly based on results.

Your SME AI Advantage Action Plan

As you consider your own AI journey, remember these key principles:

Embrace Your Constraints: Your limited budget and resources will force you to make better, more focused decisions than companies with unlimited resources.

Move Fast: Your ability to make quick decisions and implement rapidly is a massive competitive advantage. Use it.

Stay Focused: Resist the temptation to solve every problem at once. Pick the most impactful issue and solve it well.

Leverage Your Relationships: Your closer customer and supplier relationships provide advantages that larger companies can't match.

Think Iteratively: Plan for continuous improvement rather than trying to build the perfect solution from day one.

Case Study 1: Retail Chain Inventory Optimisation Revolution (illustrative)

The Company Garden Centre Group, a family-owned chain of 12 garden centres across the Midlands with 95 employees, was struggling with inventory management. Seasonal demand variations, perishable products, and weather dependencies made traditional inventory planning ineffective.

The Challenge: The company was experiencing

- 15% of products regularly out of stock during peak seasons
- £200,000 in annual waste from unsold perishable items
- 23% of warehouse space occupied by slow-moving inventory
- Manual ordering processes taking 8 hours per week per location
- Inability to respond quickly to weather-driven demand changes

The Enterprise Alternative: A large competitor had spent £800,000 on an enterprise resource planning system with AI capabilities. The implementation took 14 months, required extensive customisation, and still didn't effectively handle seasonal variations or weather impacts.

The SME Advantage Approach: Working with the company's operations manager and three store managers, we implemented a focused AI solution in just 6 weeks:

Week 1-2: Data collection and analysis

- Gathered 3 years of sales data, weather records, and seasonal patterns
- Identified the top 200 products that represented 70% of revenue

Week 3-4: Solution deployment

- Implemented a cloud-based demand forecasting system
- Integrated with existing point-of-sale systems

- Trained the AI on historical data and seasonal patterns

Week 5 6: Testing and refinement

- Ran parallel ordering systems for validation
- Adjusted algorithms based on manager feedback
- Trained staff on the new system

The Results After 12 Months

- Stockouts reduced from 15% to 4%
- Waste decreased by 60%, saving £120,000 annually
- Inventory turns improved from 4.2 to 6.1 times per year
- Ordering time reduced from 8 hours to 2 hours per week per location
- Revenue increased by 12% due to better product availability
- The system paid for itself within 4 months

The SME Success Factors

- **Speed**: Decision made in one meeting, implemented in 6 weeks
- **Focus**: Concentrated on the 200 products that mattered most
- **Flexibility**: Could quickly adjust algorithms based on real-world feedback
- **Direct involvement**: Store managers helped design and test the solution
- **Iterative improvement**: System gets better with each season of data

Key Lesson: While the large competitor spent 20 times more on a complex solution, the SME achieved better results faster by focusing on their specific needs and leveraging their agility.

Case Study 2: Micro Manufacturing Smart Quality Control (illustrative)

The company Precision Instruments Ltd, a 7-person speciality electronics manufacturer in Bristol, produces custom sensors for marine applications. Founded by two former engineers, the company was struggling with quality control as orders increased beyond what manual inspection could handle effectively.

The Challenge

- Manual inspection of every component taking 45 minutes per unit
- 2.8% defect rate reaching customers despite inspection
- Quality control consuming 30% of production time
- Unable to scale production without hiring additional QC staff
- Inconsistent inspection standards between different team members
- Customer complaints averaging 3 4 per month

The Micro Business Reality With only 7 staff and annual revenue of £450,000, hiring additional quality control personnel wasn't financially viable. Traditional enterprise solutions requiring dedicated IT staff or extensive training were completely out of reach.

The Focused Solution Month 1: Assessment and tool selection

- Implemented Cognex In-Sight 2000 vision system (£3,200 one-time cost)
- Used IFTTT Pro (£3.99/month) to connect with existing inventory system
- Added basic Slack integration (free) for quality alerts

Month 2: Setup and training

- Trained the vision system using 200 sample components (good and defective)

- Created simple pass/fail workflows
- Set up automated alerts for quality issues

The Results After 6 Months

- Inspection time reduced from 45 minutes to 3 minutes per unit
- The defect rate dropped from 2.8% to 0.6%
- Production capacity increased by 35% without additional staff
- Customer complaints reduced to fewer than 1 per month
- Quality consistency improved significantly across all inspectors
- **Total cost: £3,224 (including setup)**
- **Annual savings: £67,000** (time savings + reduced rework)
- **ROI: 2,078% in first year**
- **Payback period: 18 days**

The Micro Business Success Factors

- **Simplicity**: single-purpose solution that required minimal training
- **Low cost**: Total investment under £3,500 vs. £50,000+ enterprise alternatives
- **Immediate impact**: Saw results within 2 weeks of installation
- **No IT dependency**: The system ran independently with minimal maintenance
- **Scalable**: Could easily add more inspection points as business grows

Key Insight: The smallest businesses often see the highest ROI from AI because they can implement focused solutions with immediate, measurable impact.

Case Study 3: Professional Services Micro Firm Client Intelligence Automation (illustrative)

The company Harris Tax Advisory, a 4-person tax consultancy in Manchester, serves high-net-worth individuals and small businesses. The founder, two senior advisors, and one administrative assistant were struggling to identify new clients and maintain relationships with existing ones.

The Challenge

- 80% of new business came from referrals, limiting growth potential
- Manual client research taking 3-4 hours per prospect
- Difficulty tracking client life events that trigger tax planning needs
- Administrative assistant spending 60% of time on client data management
- Unable to proactively identify tax-saving opportunities for existing clients
- Missing opportunities due to lack of systematic client monitoring

The Small Firm Constraints

- Annual revenue of £280,000 with tight margins
- No dedicated marketing budget or staff
- Limited time for business development activities
- Need for immediate ROI to justify any investment
- Requirement for tools that non-technical staff could use

The Streamlined Solution

Month 1: Basic automation setup

- Implemented Zapier Professional (£19.99/month) to connect existing systems
- Added LinkedIn Sales Navigator Core (£59.99/month) for prospect research
- Used ChatGPT Plus (£20/month) for client research summaries
- Set up Google Alerts (free) for client company monitoring

Month 2: Enhanced intelligence

- Added Calendly (£8/month) with automated scheduling
- Implemented Airtable Pro (£20/month) as client intelligence database
- Used Mailchimp Essentials (£10/month) for automated client newsletters
- Connected everything through Zapier workflows

Month 3: Optimization and scaling

- Added Typeform Pro (£25/month) for client data collection
- Implemented simple reporting dashboards
- Created automated client check-in sequences

Total monthly cost: £162.98 Setup time: 3 months (working 2 hours per week)

The Transformation Results After 12 Months

- New client acquisition increased by 150% (from 8 to 20 new clients annually)
- Client research time reduced from 3-4 hours to 30 minutes per prospect
- Administrative time for client management reduced by 70%
- Identified £89,000 in additional tax-saving opportunities for existing clients
- Client retention improved from 85% to 96%
- Average client value increased by 40% due to proactive planning
- **Annual subscription cost: £1,956**
- **Additional revenue generated: £156,000**
- **ROI: 7,877% in first year**
- **Payback period: 4.6 days**

The Micro Firm Advantages

- **Rapid implementation**: No committee approvals or IT department delays
- **Personal touch**: AI enhanced rather than replaced personal relationships
- **Immediate feedback**: Could adjust strategies based on real-time results
- **Cost-effective**: Used consumer-grade tools rather than enterprise solutions
- **Flexible scaling**: Could add or remove tools based on actual usage

Key Success Factors

- Started with free/low-cost tools to prove the concept.
- Focused on augmenting existing strengths rather than replacing them
- Measured everything to justify continued investment
- Used existing relationships and referrals more systematically
- Kept solutions simple enough for non-technical staff to manage

The Competitive Edge Created The firm now competes effectively against much larger tax advisory firms by:

- Responding to prospects within hours rather than days
- Providing more comprehensive client intelligence and proactive advice
- Maintaining systematic client relationships that larger firms can't match
- Operating with higher margins due to increased efficiency

Replicable Lessons for Other Micro Businesses

1. **Start with workflow automation** before investing in complex AI
2. **Use consumer tools creatively** rather than expensive business solutions
3. **Focus on time-saving** rather than trying to revolutionize your business
4. **Measure everything** to justify each tool's continued use
5. **Build incrementally.** add one tool at a time and optimize before adding more

In summary:

SMEs are uniquely positioned to capitalise on AI's agility, affordability, and impact. By focusing on practical, immediate applications and leveraging their inherent flexibility, smaller businesses can outpace larger competitors bogged down by complexity and inertia. The key is to start small, move fast, and build on each success, turning your size into your greatest AI advantage.

In the next chapter, we'll explore how to identify and prioritise the AI opportunities that will deliver the greatest impact for your specific business. But first, take a moment to appreciate the unique advantages you possess as an SME. While your larger competitors are still forming committees to discuss AI strategy, you can be implementing solutions that drive real business value.

Your size isn't a limitation – it's your competitive edge in the AI revolution.

CHAPTER 3

AI Business Impact Framework

A Simple Methodology for Identifying High-Value AI Opportunities

The challenge isn't whether AI can help your business; it's knowing where to start. Too many SMEs dive into AI implementation without a clear strategy, leading to wasted resources and disappointing results. The AI Business Impact Framework provides a systematic approach to identify, evaluate, and prioritise AI opportunities that deliver measurable business value.

Why a Structured Framework Matters

The rapid democratisation of AI means SMEs now have access to powerful tools once reserved for large enterprises. However, this abundance also brings risk: without a clear framework, SMEs can fall prey to "shiny object syndrome", investing in tools that don't align with their business needs or capabilities. Consulting models like McKinsey's "Three Horizons of Growth" and the Resource Orchestration Theory (RO) highlight the importance of aligning technology adoption with organisational strategy, resource readiness, and change management capacity.

Why Use a Framework?

- Reduces risk: By systematically assessing opportunities, SMEs avoid wasted investment and focus on high-impact areas.
- Builds consensus: A transparent process helps align stakeholders and manage expectations.
- Accelerates learning: Structured pilots and phased rollouts enable rapid iteration and scaling of what works.

Models to support the framework

- Resource Orchestration Theory (RO): Emphasises aligning and mobilising resources (people, data, tech) for successful AI adoption.
- McKinsey's Three Horizons of Growth: Encourages balancing short-term wins with long-term innovation.
- Kotter's 8-Step Change Model: Underlines the importance of urgency, coalition-building, and quick wins in driving adoption.
- Balanced Scorecard: Ensures alignment of AI initiatives with strategic business objectives.

This framework cuts through the complexity and hype, giving you a practical roadmap to make informed decisions about where AI can create the biggest impact in your organisation.

The Four Pillar Assessment Model

The AI Business Impact Framework rests on four fundamental pillars that help you evaluate potential AI opportunities systematically:

Before You Start: Build a Cross-Functional AI Taskforce

- Form a small, empowered team representing key business functions (operations, sales, finance, IT). This ensures diverse perspectives and

faster decision-making, echoing the "Direct Stakeholder Involvement" advantage from Chapter 2.
- Assign an AI Champion—someone responsible for driving the process, tracking progress, and communicating wins and lessons learnt.

Pillar 1: Pain Point Analysis

Start by identifying your organisation's most pressing challenges. These fall into four categories that directly impact your bottom line:

Cost reduction opportunities look at repetitive tasks consuming significant employee time, manual processes prone to errors, and areas where you're paying for external services that could be automated. Consider your accounts department spending hours on invoice processing or customer service teams answering the same questions repeatedly.

Efficiency Gaps reveal themselves through bottlenecks in your workflows, inconsistent processes across teams, and delays in decision-making due to lack of real-time information. These might include project management challenges, inventory management issues, or communication breakdowns between departments.

Customer Experience Friction appears as slow response times to customer enquiries, inconsistent service quality, difficulty in personalising customer interactions, and challenges in understanding customer needs and preferences.

Revenue Growth Constraints manifest as difficulty identifying new sales opportunities, challenges in lead qualification and nurturing, limited ability to cross-sell or upsell, and lack of insights into market trends and customer behaviour.

Pillar 1: Pain Point Analysis (Action Steps)

- Conduct a "Pain Point Workshop": Use simple tools like sticky notes or digital whiteboards (Miro, Mural) to gather input from staff on daily frustrations and bottlenecks.
- Map pain points to value streams: Apply the Lean Six Sigma "Value Stream Mapping" approach to visualise where inefficiencies or delays occur.
- Prioritise by business impact: Use the Eisenhower Matrix to distinguish urgent/important issues from less critical ones.

Example:
A 20-person logistics SME identified that 30% of customer service time was spent on tracking shipments. By mapping this pain point, they targeted AI-powered tracking bots, freeing staff for higher-value work.

Pillar 2: Data Readiness Assessment

AI thrives on data, but not all data is created equal. Evaluate your organisation's data landscape across three dimensions:

Data availability requires you to catalogue what data you currently collect, identify gaps in data collection, and assess whether you have sufficient historical data for meaningful analysis. Many SMEs are surprised to discover they're already sitting on valuable data goldmines.

Data quality involves examining the accuracy and completeness of your data, consistency across different systems, and how up-to-date your information is. Poor data quality is the fastest way to derail an AI project.

Data accessibility looks at how easily you can access and integrate data from different sources, whether data is trapped in silos, and what technical capabilities you have for data extraction and processing.

Pillar 2: Data Readiness Assessment (Action Steps)

- Run a "Data Audit Sprint": catalogue all existing data sources (spreadsheets, CRM, emails, etc.), noting gaps and inconsistencies.
- Score data quality: Use a simple 1–5 scale for accuracy, completeness, and accessibility for each key data set.
- Set a "data hygiene" goal: Assign owners to clean and standardise data before starting any AI project.

Consulting Tip:
Adopt the "Data Maturity Model" (Gartner) to benchmark your current state and set realistic improvement targets.

Pillar 3: Implementation Complexity Evaluation

Not all AI solutions are created equal in terms of implementation difficulty. Assess opportunities using these criteria:

Technical complexity ranges from simple plug-and-play solutions to custom development requirements. Start with low-complexity solutions that can deliver quick wins while building your organisation's AI confidence and capabilities.

Change management requirements Consider how much training staff will need, whether processes need to be redesigned, and the level of resistance you might encounter. The most technically perfect solution will fail if your team won't adopt it.

Resource requirements encompass initial investment costs, ongoing operational expenses, and the internal time and expertise needed for implementation and maintenance.

Pillar 3: Implementation Complexity Evaluation (Action Steps)

- Use a Complexity-Impact Matrix: Plot each AI opportunity by "Implementation Complexity" (low to high) vs. "Expected Impact" (low to high). Start with low-complexity, high-impact projects.
- Pilot with off-the-shelf tools: Tools like Zapier, n8n, or Tidio allow SMEs to test AI applications with minimal risk and investment.
- Plan for change management: apply Kotter's 8-Step Change Model, create urgency, build a guiding coalition, and generate quick wins to build momentum.

Example:

A 35-person engineering firm piloted an AI-powered invoice processing tool using Zapier and QuickBooks, requiring only a half-day staff training session and resulting in a 60% reduction in processing errors.

Pillar 4: Business Impact Potential

Finally, evaluate each opportunity based on its potential to deliver measurable business value:

Quantifiable benefits should be expressed in specific terms—hours saved, error rates reduced, customer satisfaction scores improved, or revenue increases. Avoid vague promises of "improved efficiency".

Strategic alignment ensures the AI initiative supports your broader business objectives and competitive positioning. An AI solution that doesn't align with your strategic direction is unlikely to receive sustained support.

Scalability potential considers whether the solution can grow with your business and be extended to other areas of your organisation.

Pillar 4: Business Impact Potential (Action Steps)

- Define SMART metrics: Make benefits Specific, Measurable, Achievable, Relevant, and Time-bound (e.g., "Reduce manual order entry by 50% in three months").
- Align with strategic goals: Use the Balanced Scorecard approach to ensure AI projects support financial, customer, process, and learning objectives.
- Assess scalability: Ask, "If this pilot works, can we roll it out to other teams or markets with minimal extra effort?"

Example:
A small retailer started with AI-driven email marketing and then scaled up to AI-powered sales forecasting after proving the initial ROI.

The Opportunity Scoring Matrix

Once you've assessed potential AI opportunities against the four pillars, use this simple scoring system to prioritise your initiatives:

Rate each opportunity from 1 to 5 across four dimensions:

- **Business Impact**: How significantly will this solve a real business problem?
- **Implementation Ease**: How straightforward is this to implement with your current resources?
- **Data Readiness**: How well prepared is your data for this application?
- **ROI Potential**: How quickly and substantially will you see returns?

Multiply the scores to get a total opportunity score (maximum 625). Focus first on opportunities scoring above 400, as these represent your highest value, lowest risk AI implementations.

Opportunity Scoring Matrix (Action Steps)

- Involve your AI taskforce in scoring: Use a shared spreadsheet or simple scoring app.
- Review quarterly: reassess priorities as new data, technologies, or business needs emerge.
- Document lessons learnt: Keep a "Project Playbook" to capture what worked, what didn't, and why.

Implementation Roadmap

Your AI journey should follow a structured progression:

Phase 1: Quick Wins (0–3 months) focuses on implementing simple, off-the-shelf AI tools that require minimal setup and deliver immediate value. These build confidence and demonstrate AI's potential to sceptical team members.

- Phase 1 (Quick Wins):
    - Identify at least one "low-hanging fruit" project (e.g., automating appointment scheduling or invoice reminders).
    - Set up a 30-day pilot with clear success criteria.
    - Share results with the whole team to build buy-in.

Phase 2: Process Enhancement (3-9 months) involves integrating AI tools into existing workflows and beginning to automate routine tasks. This phase starts delivering substantial efficiency gains.

- Phase 2 (Process Enhancement):
    - Integrate AI tools with existing workflows (e.g., connect your CRM to your email marketing platform).
    - Provide short, targeted training sessions for staff.

Phase 3: Strategic Integration (6–18 months) sees AI becoming embedded in core business processes, with custom solutions developed for specific needs and AI insights driving strategic decisions.

- Phase 3 (Strategic Integration):
    - Develop custom AI solutions or deeper integrations as your confidence and data maturity grow.
    - Involve leadership in reviewing how AI insights are shaping business strategy.

Phase 4: AI-Driven Innovation (12+ months) transforms your business model, with AI enabling new products or services and creating sustainable competitive advantages.

- Phase 4 (AI-Driven Innovation):
    - Explore new business models enabled by AI (e.g., subscription services, predictive maintenance offerings).
    - Participate in regulatory sandboxes or industry forums to stay ahead of compliance and best practices.

Practical Tools and Costs for SMEs

Understanding the AI tool landscape helps you make informed decisions about implementation:

Free Tier options provide excellent starting points:

- ChatGPT Free: Content creation, brainstorming, basic analysis
- Google Analytics Intelligence: Automated insights from website data
- Calendly: AI-powered scheduling optimization
- Canva AI: Design assistance and content generation

Low-Cost Solutions (£10 100/month):

- Grammarly Business (£12.50/user/month): Writing assistance and brand consistency
- HubSpot Starter with AI features (£15/month): CRM with predictive lead scoring
- Mailchimp with AI (£35/month): Email marketing optimization
- Microsoft 365 Copilot (£24/user/month): AI across Office applications

Mid-Range Solutions (£100 1000/month):

- Salesforce Einstein (£200+/month): Advanced CRM AI capabilities
- Intercom Resolution Bot (£400/month): Sophisticated customer service automation
- Tableau with AI features (£600/month): Advanced data analytics and insights
- Monday.com with AI (£300/month): Project management with predictive features

Enterprise Solutions (£1000+/month):

- Custom machine learning platforms
- Industry-specific AI solutions
- Advanced predictive analytics systems

Getting Started: Your First 30 Days

Week 1 2: Conduct your assessment using the four-pillar framework. Involve key team members in identifying pain points and evaluating your data readiness.

Week 3: Score your opportunities using the matrix and select your top 2 to 3 initiatives for Phase 1 implementation.

Week 4: Begin implementing your first AI tool, starting with the highest scoring, lowest complexity opportunity.

The key to successful AI implementation isn't choosing the most advanced technology; it's selecting solutions that solve real business problems while fitting your organisation's current capabilities and constraints. Start small, measure results, and build confidence before tackling more complex implementations.

Your AI journey begins with understanding where you are today and taking the first practical step forward. The framework provides the roadmap; your commitment to systematic evaluation and gradual implementation will determine your success.

Case Study 1: Local Marketing Agency (8 Staff) (illustrative)

Background: Creative Spark, a digital marketing agency in Manchester, struggled with proposal writing, social media content creation, and client reporting—tasks that consumed 40% of their billable time.

Assessment Using the Framework:

- **Pain Points**: High-value staff spending excessive time on repetitive tasks, inconsistent proposal quality, and delayed client reports affecting customer satisfaction
- **Data Readiness**: Good client performance data, extensive content libraries, but information scattered across multiple tools
- **Implementation Complexity**: Low—existing tools with AI features available
- **Business Impact**: High potential for cost savings and improved client satisfaction

Solution Implementation: The agency implemented a three-tool approach costing £180 monthly:

Jasper AI (£49/month) transformed their content creation process. Instead of spending 8 hours weekly crafting social media posts, they now generate monthlong content calendars in 2 hours, with team members focusing on strategy and client relationships.

Notion AI (£96/month for the team) revolutionised their proposal process. Template-based proposals now take 45 minutes instead of 4 hours, with consistent quality and personalisation that impressed clients.

Zapier automation (£35/month) connected their project management system to reporting tools, automatically generating client reports that previously required manual compilation.

Results After 6 Months:

- 22 hours weekly saved across the team (equivalent to £15,400 monthly at their average hourly rate)
- 35% faster proposal turnaround, resulting in 12% higher conversion rates
- Client satisfaction scores improved from 7.2 to 8.6 out of 10
- Two additional clients taken on without hiring extra staff
- ROI of 8,400% on AI tool investment

Key Success Factors: Started with familiar tools, focused on tasks everyone found frustrating, and involved the whole team in identifying opportunities.

Case Study 2: Manufacturing Company (150 Staff) (illustrative)

Background: Precision Parts Ltd, a precision engineering company in Birmingham, faced challenges with quality control, inventory management, and customer service across their growing operation.

Assessment Using the Framework:

- **Pain Points**: 3% defect rate costing £180K annually, inventory holding costs 25% above industry average, customer inquiries taking 48 hours average response time
- **Data Readiness**: Strong production data from machinery, good inventory records, but customer data fragmented
- **Implementation Complexity**: Medium—required integration work but no custom development
- **Business Impact**: Potential for significant cost savings and revenue protection

Solution Implementation: The company implemented a phased approach over 12 months, investing £42,000 in total:

Phase 1: Customer Service AI Zendesk with Answer Bot (£299/month) handled 60% of routine customer enquiries automatically, reducing response times from 48 hours to under 2 hours for complex queries.

Phase 2: Quality Control Enhancement Cognex In-Sight cameras with AI (£25,000 one time) integrated into production lines, using computer vision to detect defects that human inspectors missed.

Phase 3: Inventory Optimisation Blue Yonder demand forecasting (£15,000 annually) analysed historical sales, seasonality, and market factors to optimise inventory levels.

Results After 12 Months:

- Defect rate reduced from 3% to 0.8%, saving £145,000 annually
- Inventory costs reduced by 18%, freeing up £320,000 in working capital
- Customer satisfaction increased from 73% to 89%
- The customer service team refocused on complex problem solving and relationship building

- Overall ROI of 780% in first year, with ongoing benefits

Key Success Factors: Phased implementation allowed for learning and adjustment, strong leadership support ensured adoption, and clear metrics tracked progress at each stage.

In summary:

A structured, consulting-informed framework empowers SMEs to identify, prioritise, and implement AI where it matters most—balancing ambition with pragmatism and ensuring every step delivers measurable business value.

PART II
STRATEGIC PLANNING

CHAPTER 4

Your AI Readiness Assessment

Evaluating Your Data, Processes, and Team Capabilities

AI isn't a one-size-fits-all solution, but nearly every SME has untapped opportunities. Let's cut through complexity with a simple 6-step framework to assess your readiness, paired with real-world examples of businesses like yours succeeding.

1. Clarify Your AI Goals and Use Cases

- Start with the business problem: Identify 1–3 high-impact areas where AI could add value (e.g., automating customer queries, improving sales forecasting, streamlining operations).
- Map to business KPIs: Ensure each potential AI use case aligns with measurable objectives, such as reducing costs, increasing efficiency, or improving customer satisfaction.

2. Assess Your Data: Quality, Accessibility, and Relevance

- Inventory your data assets: List where your key business data lives (spreadsheets, CRM, accounting software, cloud storage).

- Check data quality: For each data source, ask:
  - Is the data accurate and up to date?
  - Are there lots of missing or inconsistent entries?
  - Is the data relevant to the AI use case you identified?

- Evaluate accessibility: Can you easily export or access the data when needed? Data locked in siloed or legacy systems may need attention.
- Keep it simple: for most SMEs, a spreadsheet-based checklist is enough—no need for specialist tools or audits at this stage.

3. Review Your IT Infrastructure

- Basic infrastructure check: Ensure you have reliable internet, up-to-date computers, and secure cloud storage.
- Cloud readiness: If you lack on-premises capacity, consider cloud-based AI tools (many offer pay-as-you-go pricing and require no upfront investment).
- Scalability: For heavier workloads, cloud GPU computing can be rented as needed, avoiding costly hardware purchases.
- Security and compliance: Confirm your data is protected and that you follow basic privacy and compliance standards relevant to your industry.

4. Evaluate Team Skills and Capacity

- Team self-assessment: Gauge your team's comfort with data analysis, digital tools, and new technologies.
- Identify gaps: If you lack in-house expertise, consider basic AI training (many free or low-cost online courses exist) or seek temporary support from managed service providers.
- Assign ownership: Designate a point person to coordinate AI readiness efforts and be the main contact for any external advisors.

5. Use SME-Focused Readiness Tools and Checklists

Several organisations offer free or low-cost AI readiness assessment tools designed for SMEs. These typically involve simple questionnaires and checklists covering data, infrastructure, and skills:

- Digital Catapult's AI Adoption Assessment Toolkit: Evaluates digital maturity across leadership, people, and technology.
- ANS Group, Ramsac, and other consultancies offer quick self-assessment surveys and practical guidance, often tailored for SMEs.
- Dialzara's AI Readiness Checklist: Focuses on infrastructure, goals, tools, team training, and monitoring ideal for SMEs starting out.

6. Pilot and Iterate

- Start small: Choose a low-risk, high-value use case and test with off-the-shelf AI tools (many have free tiers or trial periods).
- Monitor results: Track performance, collect feedback, and refine your approach before scaling up.

Sample SME AI Readiness Checklist

Area	Key Questions	Action if Gaps Found
Data Quality	Is your data accurate, complete, and up-to-date?	Clean up data; set data entry rules
Data Accessibility	Can you access/export the data you need?	Move to cloud/shared systems
Infrastructure	Is your IT setup reliable and secure?	Upgrade basics; use cloud tools

| Team Skills | Does your team understand basic digital tools? | Provide basic AI/data training |
| Use Case Fit | Does your data support your chosen AI use case? | Collect missing data; adjust goals |

Resource Smart Tips for SMEs

- Leverage existing tools: Many business platforms (e.g., Microsoft 365, Zoho, QuickBooks) now include basic AI features at no extra cost—use these for initial pilots.
- Avoid overengineering: Don't aim for "perfect" data or infrastructure. Good enough is often sufficient to start and learn.
- Seek external support only as needed: Managed service providers or consultants can fill gaps for a limited period, reducing the need for permanent hires. Focus on upskilling your own staff for the long term.
- Continuous improvement: Treat AI readiness as an ongoing process—review and update your checklist quarterly as your business and technology evolve.

SME AI Stack (Cost Optimized)

Function	Free Tier	Paid Tier (Best Value)
Writing	Grammarly	Jasper (£39/mo)
Design	Canva	Adobe Express (£9.99/mo)
CRM	Zoho CRM Free	HubSpot Starter (£41/mo)
Finance	Wave Accounting	QuickBooks (£12/mo)

Key Takeaway: AI readiness isn't about having perfect data or PhD staff – it's about strategically applying accessible tools to your unique pain points. Start small, measure obsessively, and let results (not hype) guide your next steps.

Data Security

A quick divergence into data security: your brand and reputation are easily lost through one ransomware attack. Companies have gone out of business, even if the actual impact was not significant.

Examples of companies that effectively ceased business after a ransomware attack and their customer data leaked.

MediSecure (2024) MediSecure, which provides electronic prescriptions in Australia, announced that it had experienced a breach that compromised the records of 12.9 million people, nearly half the population of the country. The attackers exploited a vulnerability to plant ransomware and encrypt sensitive patient data. Following the incident, MediSecure requested a financial bailout from the Australian government, presumably to protect itself against the potential of lawsuits from affected parties seeking to hold the company responsible for the exposure of their personal information. The government declined the request, and shortly after, MediSecure entered a state called "administration", which effectively means that it is being reorganised and may cease operations once it finishes responding to the fallout from the breach.

National Public Data (2024) In August 2024, National Public Data, which collects and processes information for background checks, announced the exposure of 2.9 billion records containing personal information associated with up to 170 million people. The attack occurred because hackers located a zip file on the company's website, giving them access to its databases. Several months later, the company filed for bankruptcy and shut down due to the financial impact of the breach.

TravelEx (2020) In early 2020 – as Covid-19 was spreading and most of the world were still enjoying the final weeks of "before times" – the foreign currency exchange company TravelEx experienced a ransomware attack that shut down its operations in 30 countries. The attackers demanded $6 million (some sources reported $3 million) in ransom to restore the company's data. The company apparently negotiated with the attackers, who agreed to settle for a payment of $2.3 million. But like the 92% of companies that pay ransoms without fully recovering their data, TravelEx wasn't able to go back to normal after settling up with the hackers. Instead, it ended up restructuring, effectively going out of business.

When integrating AI, **data security and privacy** should be a top priority for SMBs. Protecting sensitive information requires strong measures in three main areas:

Security Area	Key Measures
Technical Protection	- Encrypt data at all stages - Use multi-factor authentication - Apply regular security updates
Operational Safeguards	- Implement access control systems - Conduct regular security audits - Develop emergency response plans
Compliance Management	- Follow regulations like GDPR/CCPA - Maintain clear data handling documentation - Perform privacy reviews

Choose AI tools that prioritise security, offer enterprise-grade features, and comply with regulations. These steps help ensure your business can safely leverage AI while safeguarding sensitive information.

Case Study 1: Micro Business (8 Employees) (illustrative)

Company: Brighton-based B2B copywriting agency
Challenge: 50% time spent on admin vs. billable work

AI Solutions Implemented:

1. Grammarly Free + ChatGPT Plus (£16/mo): Draft client proposals 3x faster
2. Calendly AI Scheduler (£8/user/mo): Reduced meeting conflicts by 70%
3. Trello Butler Automation (Free): Auto-assign tasks based on keywords

Results (3 Months):

- 28% more client projects delivered
- £12k saved by avoiding freelance overflow
- Team satisfaction up 35% (less grind work)

Key Insight: "We started with tools we already knew – no complex integrations." – Founder

Case Study 2: Scaling SME (180 Employees) (illustrative)

Company: Midlands industrial equipment manufacturer
Challenge: Inconsistent inventory forecasting causing £220k/year in waste

AI Solutions Implemented:

1. Microsoft 365 Copilot (£24/user/mo): Analyze 5 years of sales data → demand predictions
2. QuickBooks AI Insights (£40/mo): Real-time cash flow alerts
3. Custom ChatGPT Plugin (£1,200 one time): Answer technical queries using product manuals

Results (6 Months):

- 18% reduction in excess stock
- 14% faster customer query resolution
- £75k annual savings from optimized procurement

Lesson Learnt: "Mid-tier tools gave 80% of enterprise AI benefits at 20% of the cost." – Operations Director

In summary:

For SMEs with limited resources, an accurate AI readiness assessment is about focusing on practical, high-impact areas: clarify your goals, check your data and infrastructure with simple tools, empower your team, and start small. Free and low-cost checklists and online tools can guide you, and incremental improvements will set you up for successful, cost-effective AI adoption.

CHAPTER 5

The Four Pillars of AI Success:

Cost Reduction, Operational Efficiency, Customer Experience, and Revenue Growth

Artificial intelligence is not just a buzzword or a distant promise for tomorrow's business giants. For small and medium enterprises (SMEs), AI is a practical, proven lever for driving real business results right now. But to move beyond the hype and realise measurable value, it's crucial to focus on four foundational pillars: cost reduction, operational efficiency, customer experience, and revenue growth. This chapter breaks down each pillar, offers actionable strategies, and illustrates them with real-world case studies from SMEs like yours.

The Four Pillars: Why They Matter for SMEs

The "Four Pillars" approach is grounded in decades of business transformation research, echoing frameworks like the Balanced Scorecard and Lean Six Sigma, which emphasise the need to balance cost, efficiency, customer focus, and growth. For SMEs, these pillars are not abstract ideals— they are the foundation for sustainable competitiveness in a world where agility and resourcefulness are more valuable than sheer scale. By focusing on these pillars, SMEs can prioritise AI investments that directly support their survival and expansion, rather than chasing technology for its own sake.

1. Cost Reduction: Doing More With Less

SMEs often operate with lean teams and tight margins. AI's automation capabilities mean that even the smallest businesses can now access efficiencies once reserved for large enterprises. According to McKinsey, automation of knowledge work is one of the largest sources of potential productivity gains for SMEs.

For SMEs, every pound or dollar saved is a pound or dollar earned. AI's ability to automate repetitive tasks, optimise resource allocation, and reduce errors can translate directly into significant cost savings. Research shows that SMEs adopting AI can achieve productivity gains of 27% to 133%, with cost reduction being a key driver.

Where there is a process, there is an opportunity for automation, and when those processes cross organisational boundaries, these are often the best cost-saving and efficiency options; an example might be a sale to order processing to fulfilment and shipping (or access if digital). This has a close link to operational efficiency, which we will see in a moment.

Practical Examples:

- Automated Customer Service: AI chatbots handle up to 90% of routine queries, freeing staff for higher-value work and reducing the need for additional hires.
- Invoice and Expense Automation: Tools like QuickBooks' AI-powered features (from £12/month) automatically categorise expenses, flag anomalies, and speed up reconciliation.
- Inventory Optimisation: AI-driven demand forecasting reduces overstock and wastage, especially in sectors like retail and hospitality.

Metrics to Track:

- Cost per customer interaction

- Reduction in overtime or temporary staffing
- Decrease in error-related losses

Pragmatic Actions for SMEs:

- Start with a Cost Audit: List your top five recurring costs (e.g., payroll, admin, customer service) and identify which are driven by repetitive manual work.
- Pilot Automation in One Area: Choose a single process—such as invoice processing or appointment scheduling—and trial an AI-powered tool for 30 days.
- Negotiate with Vendors: Many SaaS providers offer SME discounts or scalable pricing. Don't be afraid to ask for a trial or a custom package.
- Monitor and Reinvest Savings: Use the money saved from automation to invest in growth areas, such as marketing or new product development.

Real-World Example: (illustrative)
A 7-person legal practice used QuickBooks AI to automate expense categorisation and reduced their monthly bookkeeping costs by 40%, allowing the office manager to focus on client onboarding.

Key Tools for SMEs (Cost Optimised):

Talking about cost optimisation, we should also look at the tools available to use 'out of the box'.

Function	Free Option	Paid Option (Best Value)
Writing/Content	Grammarly	Jasper (£39/month)
Scheduling	Calendly Free	Calendly AI (£8/user/month)

CRM/Sales	HubSpot Free	HubSpot Starter (£41/month)
Finance	Wave Accounting	QuickBooks (£12/month)
Automation	Zapier Free	Zapier (£20/month)
Design	Canva Free	Canva Pro (£10.99/month)

2. Operational Efficiency: Streamlining the Everyday

Operational inefficiency is a silent profit killer for SMEs. Consulting models like Lean highlight that eliminating waste (time, errors, unnecessary steps) is the fastest way to boost profitability. AI, with its ability to "connect the dots" across systems, is a natural fit for this mission. Operational bottlenecks and manual processes can quietly drain SME resources. AI's strength lies in automating the "invisible work", from scheduling and workflow management to document processing and compliance checks.

Practical Examples:

- Workflow Automation: Zapier (free tier available, paid from £20/month) connects your apps and automates tasks like data entry, appointment reminders, and lead routing.
- HR Process Automation: ChatGPT-based tools draft job descriptions, screen CVs, and even schedule interviews, reducing HR admin by up to 60%.
- Predictive Maintenance: For manufacturing SMEs, AI sensors predict equipment failures before they happen, minimising downtime and maintenance costs.

Metrics to Track:

- Time saved per process
- Increase in tasks completed per staff member
- Reduction in process cycle times

Pragmatic Actions for SMEs:

- Map Your Processes: Use simple flowcharts or tools like Lucidchart to visualise where time and effort are wasted.
- Automate Integrations: Use Zapier or n8n to connect your CRM, email, and calendar, eliminating manual data entry and reducing errors.
- Adopt Predictive Tools: For SMEs in manufacturing or logistics, start with low-cost IoT sensors and AI dashboards to predict maintenance needs or delivery delays.
- Review Regularly: Set a quarterly "efficiency review" to identify new automation opportunities as your business evolves.

Real-World Example: (illustrative)
A 25-employee logistics firm implemented Zapier to automate order updates between their website, CRM, and warehouse system, cutting manual processing time by 70%.

3. Customer Experience: Delight at Scale

Customer experience is a key differentiator for SMEs. Research from Bain & Company shows that companies excelling in customer experience grow revenues 4–8% above their market. AI allows SMEs to deliver "big company" service without big company resources. AI empowers SMEs to deliver personalised, responsive service that rivals or even surpasses big brands. From 24/7 chatbots to AI-driven recommendations, the technology enables you to anticipate needs and resolve issues faster.

Practical Examples:

- AI Chatbots: Tools like Dialzara or ManyChat (free and paid plans) provide instant answers, resolve common issues, and escalate complex queries to humans only when needed.
- Personalised Marketing: Jasper AI (from £39/month) generates customised email and ad copy, while Canva's AI suggests design tweaks that boost engagement.
- Customer Feedback Analysis: AI tools analyse reviews and survey responses, surfacing actionable insights for continuous improvement.

Metrics to Track:

- Customer satisfaction (CSAT) and Net Promoter Scores (NPS)
- First contact resolution rate
- Response and handling times

Pragmatic Actions for SMEs:

- Deploy a Chatbot: Start with a free or low-cost chatbot on your website or Facebook page to handle FAQs and collect leads.
- Personalise Outreach: Use AI tools in your email platform (like Mailchimp or HubSpot) to segment customers and send tailored messages.
- Analyse Feedback: Use AI-powered sentiment analysis tools (e.g., MonkeyLearn) to quickly interpret customer reviews and spot trends.
- Train Staff on AI Tools: Make sure your team knows how to use AI-driven insights to personalise their interactions and resolve issues faster.

Real-World Example: (illustrative)
A boutique hotel with 12 staff used ManyChat to automate guest communications, achieving a 25% increase in direct bookings and a 30% improvement in guest satisfaction scores.

4. Revenue Growth: Unlocking New Opportunities

AI isn't just about doing the same things faster; it's about discovering new ways to grow. Consulting models like the Ansoff Matrix encourage businesses to use technology to unlock new markets, products, and revenue streams. Perhaps the most exciting pillar of AI is that it doesn't just save money; it helps you make more. By identifying new sales opportunities, optimising pricing, and enabling smarter marketing, AI becomes a growth engine for SMEs.

Practical Examples:

- Sales Forecasting: HubSpot's AI-powered CRM (free and paid plans) predicts deal closures, helping sales teams focus on the most promising leads.
- Dynamic Pricing: Tools like Prisync (from £39/month) adjust prices in real time based on market demand and competitor activity.
- Cross Selling/Upselling: AI analyses customer purchase history to suggest relevant add-ons, increasing average order value.

Metrics to Track:

- Revenue per customer
- Conversion and upsell rates
- Marketing ROI

Pragmatic Actions for SMEs:

- Implement AI-Driven Lead Scoring: Use your CRM's AI features to prioritise leads most likely to convert, focusing your sales team's efforts.
- Experiment with Dynamic Pricing: Pilot a dynamic pricing tool for a subset of products or services and monitor the impact on sales and margins.
- Upsell with AI Recommendations: Add a recommendation engine to your e-commerce platform to increase average order value.
- Track and Optimise: Use analytics to monitor which AI-driven initiatives yield the highest ROI and double down on what works.

Making the Four Pillars Work for You

Start Small, Scale Fast:
Begin with one or two pain points, such as automating customer queries or improving inventory management using off-the-shelf tools. Measure the impact using clear metrics (cost, time, satisfaction, revenue), then expand to other areas as you build confidence and capability. 256.

Monitor and Optimise:
Track key AI metrics: accuracy, speed, resolution rates, customer satisfaction, and cost efficiency. Use dashboards or built-in analytics to spot trends and areas for improvement.

Empower Your Team:
AI works best when it augments your people, not replaces them. Involve staff in tool selection, provide basic training, and encourage feedback to ensure smooth adoption.

Invest in Data Quality:
The most successful SMEs invest in data management. Clean, relevant, and accessible data is the foundation for all four pillars. Start with what you have,

then improve over time. You will hear me talk about data quality many times; it's a clear foundation.

Real-World Example: (illustrative)
A small online retailer added Prisync for dynamic pricing and saw a 12% uplift in monthly sales within the first quarter, with no increase in advertising spend.

Case Study 1: Micro Business (Under 10 Staff) (illustrative)

Company: "Bright Copy", a B2B Copywriting Agency (8 employees, London)

Challenge:
Half the team's time was lost to admin—scheduling, invoicing, and repetitive client queries—leaving little room for creative, billable work.

AI Solutions Implemented:

- ChatGPT Plus (£16/month): Draughted first versions of proposals and client emails, cutting writing time by 60%.
- Calendly AI Scheduler (£8/user/month): Automated meeting bookings, reducing back-and-forth emails.
- Trello Butler Automation (Free): Auto-assigned tasks and reminders based on project status.

Results (6 months):
- 28% more client projects delivered without increasing headcount.
- £12,000 saved by reducing reliance on freelance overflow.
- Team satisfaction scores are up 35%.

Takeaway:
Starting with easy-to-integrate, low-cost tools, Bright Copy rapidly improved efficiency and profitability, demonstrating that even the smallest teams can realise big AI wins.

Case Study 2: Scaling SME (Under 200 Staff) (illustrative)

Company: "Midlands Industrial Solutions", Equipment Manufacturer (180 employees, UK)

Challenge:
Inconsistent inventory forecasting led to £220,000/year in excess stock and frequent stockouts, frustrating customers and tying up cash.

AI Solutions Implemented:

- Microsoft 365 Copilot (£24/user/month): Analysed five years of sales and inventory data to predict demand and optimise ordering.
- QuickBooks AI Insights (£40/month): Provided real-time cash flow alerts, enabling smarter procurement decisions.
- Custom ChatGPT Plugin (£1,200 one-off): Automated responses to technical product queries, reducing support workload.

Results (6 months):

- 18% reduction in excess inventory, freeing up £40,000 in working capital.
- 14% faster customer query resolution, boosting customer satisfaction.
- £75,000 annual savings from optimised procurement and reduced waste.

Takeaway:
By layering affordable AI tools on top of existing systems, Midlands Industrial Solutions achieved enterprise-level efficiency gains at a fraction of the cost, proving that AI-driven transformation is within reach for growing SMEs.

Summary Table: Action Steps for Each Pillar

Pillar	Quick Win Action	Tool Example	Key Metric
Cost Reduction	Automate expense processing	QuickBooks AI	Cost per transaction
Operational Efficiency	Automate order updates	Zapier/n8n	Time saved per process
Customer Experience	Deploy a website chatbot	ManyChat, Dialzara	CSAT, response time
Revenue Growth	Add AI recommendations to shop	Prisync, HubSpot AI	Revenue per customer

By systematically addressing each pillar, SMEs can build a resilient, future-ready business that leverages AI for tangible, measurable results.

Conclusion

AI is no longer the preserve of tech giants. For SMEs, it's a practical toolkit for cutting costs, boosting efficiency, delighting customers, and driving new revenue. By focusing on these four pillars and learning from peers who've succeeded, you can unlock AI's full potential for your business, starting today.

By anchoring your AI journey in these four pillars, you'll ensure every investment is practical, measurable, and directly connected to your business's growth and resilience.

CHAPTER 6

Building Your AI Strategy Roadmap

Prioritising Initiatives and Creating a 12-18 Month Implementation Plan

In today's business climate, small and medium enterprises (SMEs) can no longer afford to treat artificial intelligence as a distant, "nice to have" innovation. AI is now a practical, affordable lever for operational improvement, customer delight, and competitive growth. Yet, the difference between success and wasted effort lies in how you plan and sequence your AI journey. This chapter provides a pragmatic, step-by-step framework for building your AI strategy roadmap, one that prioritises the right initiatives, aligns with your business goals, and delivers results within 12 to 18 months.

Many SMEs hesitate to adopt AI, fearing high costs, technical complexity, or disruption to daily operations. In reality, the most successful AI journeys are not about radical overnight transformation but about incremental, well-prioritised steps that match your business's unique needs and resources. A phased roadmap helps SMEs avoid common pitfalls such as over-investing in the wrong tools, underestimating change management, or failing to measure impact by ensuring each initiative is grounded in business value and feasibility.

Consulting models like the "AI Adoption Framework: Six Essential Strategies for SMEs" (Synergy) emphasise the importance of rapid experimentation, cross-functional collaboration, and continuous learning. These principles underpin the roadmap below, making AI adoption both manageable and impactful for SMEs.

The SME AI Roadmap: A Phased Approach

The most successful SME AI strategies are not grand, multi-year blueprints that gather dust. Instead, they are living roadmaps: practical, phased, and focused on incremental value delivery. Here's how to build yours:

Phase 1: Assessment & Readiness (Months 0–3)

This phase is about understanding where you are and what you need. Many SMEs already have valuable data and motivated staff; they just need to clarify priorities and build basic AI awareness.

Objective: Evaluate your current capabilities, data, and team.

Actions:

- Clarify business priorities: what are your top pain points or growth opportunities – cost, efficiency, customer experience, or new revenue streams?
- Map existing data: What data do you already collect? Is it accessible, clean, and relevant to your goals?
- Skill gap analysis: Who are your "AI champions"? Where do you need upskilling or external support?
- Quick win identification: List 2–3 processes ripe for automation or AI enhancement (e.g., customer queries, invoice processing).

Pragmatic Actions:

- Host an AI Awareness Workshop: Brief your team on what AI is (and isn't), using real SME case studies from your sector. Invite questions and gather initial ideas.

- Conduct a Pain Point Survey: Use a simple Google Form or team meeting to collect staff input on daily challenges and repetitive tasks.
- Data Audit Checklist: Create a shared spreadsheet listing all data sources (e.g., CRM, spreadsheets, emails) and score each for accessibility and quality.
- Skill Inventory: Identify staff with digital or analytical skills who could become "AI champions". Consider free online AI literacy courses for quick upskilling.
- Set a Realistic Starting Point: Choose processes that are repetitive, rules-based, and already have some digital data—these are ideal for early AI pilots.

Tip: Don't aim for perfection. Focus on what's "good enough" to start, using existing data and off-the-shelf tools.

Phase 2: Planning & Prioritisation (Months 3–6)

This stage is about focus and feasibility. Rather than spreading resources thin, successful SMEs zero in on one or two high-impact, low-complexity use cases.

Objective: Build a prioritised, budget-conscious AI plan.

Actions:

- Score potential use cases: evaluate each by business impact, feasibility, and speed of implementation.
- Select your pilot: Choose one initiative with clear value, measurable KPIs, and minimal risk (e.g., automating customer service with a chatbot).
- Budget and governance: Allocate resources, set timelines, and define who owns delivery and oversight.

Pragmatic Actions:

- Use a Scoring Matrix: Rate each potential AI use case on business impact, ease of implementation, data readiness, and ROI potential. Focus on those with the highest combined score.
- Engage Stakeholders Early: Involve end users in selecting the pilot project to ensure buy-in and practical requirements are met.
- Budget Planning: Get clear on total costs (software, training, integration) and set aside a small "experimentation fund" for rapid pilots.
- Governance Light: Assign a project owner and set up a simple reporting process—weekly check-ins and a shared dashboard—to keep the project on track.

Tip: Use a simple scoring matrix to compare use cases—prioritise those with high impact and low complexity.

Phase 3: Pilot Implementation (Months 6–9)

Pilots are about learning, not perfection. The goal is to validate value quickly, gather feedback, and build internal confidence before scaling.

Objective: Validate AI feasibility and value with a small-scale pilot.

Actions:

- Choose the right tool: Start with affordable, off-the-shelf solutions (e.g., ChatGPT Plus, QuickBooks AI, Zapier).
- Define success metrics: e.g., "Reduce customer response time by 30%", "Cut manual invoice errors by half."
- Engage the team: Involve end users early, provide basic training, and communicate the benefits.
- Monitor and iterate: collect feedback, measure results, and refine the process.

Pragmatic Actions:

- Choose Plug-and-Play Tools: Start with tools that require minimal setup, such as ChatGPT Plus for customer queries or Zapier for workflow automation.
- Define Success Metrics: Set 2–3 clear KPIs (e.g., "Reduce manual invoice errors by 50% in 3 months").
- Communicate Progress: Share early results, both wins and lessons learnt, with the wider team to maintain momentum.
- Iterate Rapidly: Use feedback loops (e.g., weekly reviews) to refine processes and address issues as they arise.

Tip: Document lessons learnt, both technical and organisational, for future scaling.

Phase 4: Scaling & Integration (Months 9–15)

Once a pilot delivers value, the next step is to expand its reach and embed AI more deeply into business processes.

Objective: Expand successful pilots across the business.

Actions:

- Roll out to new teams or processes: e.g., extend chatbots to sales, add AI-powered analytics to finance.
- Integrate with existing systems: Use APIs or automation tools to connect AI solutions to your workflow.
- Upskill staff: Offer targeted training to build confidence and capability.
- Review and update governance: Ensure compliance, transparency, and data security as you scale.

Pragmatic Actions:

- Document and Standardise: Create step-by-step guides and checklists to help other teams replicate the pilot's success.
- API Integration: Use automation tools (Zapier, n8n) to connect new AI solutions with your existing systems, reducing manual work and errors.
- Upskill at Scale: Offer targeted training to new users using short video tutorials or lunch-and-learn sessions.
- Review Compliance: As AI adoption grows, revisit data security and privacy policies to ensure ongoing compliance with regulations.

Tip: Focus on "adjacent" win areas similar to your pilot, where you can replicate success quickly.

Phase 5: Optimisation & Innovation (Months 15–18)

AI is not a "set and forget" investment. Ongoing monitoring and a culture of experimentation are key to sustaining value and uncovering new opportunities.

Objective: Continuously improve AI models and explore new use cases.

Actions:

- Monitor performance: Use dashboards to track KPIs and spot new opportunities.
- Solicit feedback: Regularly gather input from staff and customers.
- Experiment: Pilot more advanced AI (e.g., predictive analytics, dynamic pricing) as your confidence grows.
- Plan for sustainability: build internal champions, document processes, and review ROI.

Pragmatic Actions:

- Establish Performance Dashboards: Use tools like Microsoft 365 Copilot or Google Analytics to track KPIs and identify trends.
- Create a Feedback Loop: Regularly solicit input from staff and customers on what's working and what could be improved.
- Test Advanced Use Cases: As confidence grows, pilot more sophisticated AI applications (e.g., predictive analytics, AI-driven pricing).
- Celebrate and Share Success: Publicly recognise teams and individuals who drive AI success; share case studies internally to inspire further innovation.
- Plan for Sustainability: Develop internal champions, document best practices, and review your AI roadmap every 6–12 months to adapt to new business needs.

Tip: Celebrate wins and share stories to build momentum and a data-driven culture.

Tools and Solutions for the SME Roadmap

Function	Free Option	Paid Option (Best Value)
Chat/Support	Tidio Free	ChatGPT Plus (£16/month)
Scheduling	Calendly Free	Calendly AI (£8/user/month)
Automation	Zapier Free	Zapier (£20/month)
Document Drafting	Google Docs AI	Jasper (£39/month)

Analytics	Google Analytics	Microsoft 365 Copilot (£24/user/month)
Finance	Wave Accounting	QuickBooks AI (£40/month)

Key Principles for a Successful AI Roadmap

- Start with business value: Anchor every initiative in clear business outcomes cost, efficiency, customer experience, or growth.
- Prioritise for impact and feasibility: use a simple scoring system to select the best starting points.
- Pilot, measure, and scale: validate value with a small project before rolling out more broadly.
- Empower your people: Invest in basic training and clear communication to build confidence and adoption.
- Leverage off-the-shelf tools: Avoid custom builds unless absolutely necessary; today's SME-friendly AI solutions are powerful and affordable.
- Review and adapt: Make your roadmap a living document, updated as you learn and grow.

Additional Tips for a Successful AI Roadmap

- Leverage External Expertise: Consider engaging an AI consultant for initial workshops or technical assessments many offer SME-friendly packages.
- Foster a Culture of Innovation: Encourage experimentation and reward initiative, even if some pilots don't succeed.
- Stay Connected: Join SME AI forums, attend webinars, and keep up with sector-specific AI trends to inform your roadmap.

- Balance Ambition with Realism: Aim for quick wins but keep an eye on long-term strategic opportunities as your AI maturity grows.

Case Study 1: Micro Business (Under 10 Staff) (illustrative)

Company: "Peak Legal", Boutique Law Firm (7 employees, Manchester)

Challenge:
Lawyers were spending up to 40% of their week on routine admin—client intake, document drafting, and appointment scheduling—leaving little time for billable work.

Roadmap in Action:

- Assessment: Mapped data (client emails, case notes) and identified admin as the main bottleneck.
- Planning: Chose to pilot an AI-powered intake chatbot (ChatGPT Plus, £16/month) and automated scheduling (Calendly AI, £8/user/month).
- Pilot: Implemented the chatbot for client queries and automated appointment booking. Defined success as a 25% reduction in admin time within three months.
- Scaling: After a successful pilot (achieving 32% time savings), they rolled out AI document drafting (Jasper, £39/month) and integrated tools with their practice management system.
- Optimisation: Regularly reviewed client feedback and automated follow-ups, freeing up even more lawyer time.

Results (12 months):

- 40% reduction in non-billable admin.
- 18% increase in client satisfaction scores.
- £9,000 saved on part-time admin support.

Lesson:
By starting with a clear pain point and layering simple, affordable AI tools, Peak Legal rapidly improved productivity and client experience—without technical hires or major disruption.

Case Study 2: Scaling SME (Under 200 Staff) (illustrative)

Company: "Northfield Manufacturing", Precision Engineering (160 employees, Midlands)

Challenge:
Manual production scheduling and reactive maintenance led to costly delays, excess inventory, and missed deadlines.

Roadmap in Action:

- Assessment: Conducted a data audit (production logs, maintenance records) and skills inventory. Identified scheduling and maintenance as key priorities.
- Planning: Prioritised predictive maintenance as the pilot (using Microsoft 365 Copilot, £24/user/month, and a custom Zapier workflow, £20/month). Set clear KPIs: reduce downtime by 20% and inventory holding costs by 15%.
- Pilot: Launched predictive maintenance on two production lines. Trained supervisors to interpret AI alerts and schedule proactive repairs.
- Scaling: Expanded predictive maintenance across all lines, then introduced AI-powered demand forecasting (QuickBooks AI, £40/month) to optimise inventory.
- Optimisation: Established monthly review meetings, upskilled managers, and integrated AI dashboards for real-time performance tracking.

Results (18 months):

- 23% reduction in production downtime.
- 17% decrease in inventory holding costs.
- £110,000 in annual savings and improved on-time delivery.

Lesson:
Northfield's stepwise approach—pilot, scale, optimise—minimised risk and maximised buy-in, delivering measurable business impact and building internal AI capability.

Conclusion

A well-structured AI strategy roadmap is your bridge from aspiration to achievement. By breaking your journey into clear, manageable phases—assessment, planning, piloting, scaling, and optimising—you can unlock the transformative power of AI, no matter your size or sector. Start small, learn fast, and build on your wins. In the rapidly evolving world of AI, the most important step is the first one—taken with purpose, pragmatism, and a focus on real business value.

By following this roadmap, SMEs can harness AI to drive efficiency, innovation, and competitive advantage—without overextending resources or risking disruption.

PART III
FUNCTIONAL APPLICATIONS

CHAPTER 7

AI in Operations - Automating the Engine Room

Process Automation, Quality Control, and Predictive Maintenance Solutions

I talked about operational efficiencies in the previous chapter; however, given its importance to any business, automating operations deserves a chapter on its own.

For small and medium enterprises (SMEs), operations are the "engine room" of the business, the place where efficiency, quality, and reliability convert directly into profit and customer satisfaction. Yet operational challenges, manual processes, inconsistent quality, and unpredictable downtime can quietly erode margins and limit growth. Artificial Intelligence (AI) is now a practical, affordable lever for SMEs to automate, optimise, and future-proof their operations. This chapter explores how AI-driven automation, quality control, and predictive maintenance can be deployed by SMEs, with a focus on pragmatic, off-the-shelf tools (including n8n for medium enterprises) and real-world case studies.

The Strategic Value of AI in SME Operations

Historically, operational automation was the domain of large corporations with deep pockets and IT resources. Today, democratised AI and affordable automation platforms have levelled the playing field. SMEs can now harness AI to not only "keep up" but leap ahead, eliminating manual bottlenecks, ensuring consistent quality, and proactively preventing costly breakdowns. Consulting frameworks like Lean and Six Sigma emphasise that operational excellence is a key driver of profitability and customer loyalty; AI supercharges these principles by enabling real-time, data-driven action.

Key Insight:
Research shows that SMEs adopting AI in operations can cut process cycle times by up to 80%, reduce error rates by over a third, and free up thousands of staff hours annually for higher-value work.

Why AI in Operations? The SME Imperative

AI is no longer the preserve of large enterprises. In 2025, over 60% of small businesses using AI report it as an effective way to streamline daily tasks, with 45% of business processes in SMEs now potentially automatable. The benefits are tangible:

- Cost efficiency: Automating routine tasks reduces labour costs and human error, freeing up resources for growth.
- Time savings: AI can save hundreds of hours annually, allowing staff to focus on strategic and creative work.
- Scalability: SMEs can now match the operational sophistication of larger competitors without the need for large IT teams.

1. Process Automation: Streamlining the Everyday

Manual processes are a hidden tax on SME productivity. According to Forrester, SMEs lose an average of 120 hours per employee per year to manual data entry alone. Automating these tasks with AI is often the fastest route to measurable ROI.

What Is It?

Process automation uses AI and workflow automation platforms to handle repetitive, rules-based tasks – think invoicing, scheduling, data entry, and customer communications. For SMEs, this means doing more with less, faster.

Practical Applications

- Invoicing and Payments: AI tools like QuickBooks and Xero automate invoice generation, payment reminders, and reconciliation, reducing manual errors and late payments.
- Scheduling and Diary Management: Tools such as Motion and Akiflow use AI to optimise daily schedules, while Calendly automates bookings and reminders.
- Email and Document Management: Levity can sort, label, and organise emails or automate data entry into business documents.
- CRM and Sales Pipeline Automation: Salesforce and HubSpot use AI to automate lead scoring, follow-ups, and sales forecasting, helping SMEs close deals faster.

Pragmatic Actions:

- Map Your Workflow: Use a simple flowchart or process mapping tool to identify repetitive, rules-based tasks ripe for automation.
- Start Small: Select one process (e.g., invoice entry, appointment reminders) and trial a free or low-cost automation tool for 30 days.

- Involve End Users: Engage the staff who perform these tasks daily in selecting and testing the tool. Their feedback will ensure smoother adoption.
- Monitor and Iterate: Track metrics such as time saved, error reduction, and staff satisfaction. Use these insights to refine and expand automation efforts.

Real-World Example: (illustrative)
An Estonian manufacturing SME automated document recognition and reconciliation with AI, reducing monthly close time from 10 days to 2 and cutting invoice processing costs by 80%.

n8n for Medium Enterprises

n8n is a powerful workflow automation platform that combines AI capabilities with business process automation. It allows SMEs, especially those with technical capacity, to build custom automations that connect cloud apps, databases, and internal systems. n8n is especially well-suited for medium-sized businesses wanting more control and scalability than basic automation tools.

- Flexible deployment: Available as a free, self-hosted Community Edition or as a cloud-hosted service from €20/month (Starter) or €50/month (Pro), with enterprise options for unlimited workflows and advanced security.
- Cost-effective: n8n charges per complete workflow execution, not per step, making it highly economical for complex automations.
- Departmental reach: Used by IT, operations, marketing, and sales teams to connect data, automate onboarding, streamline HR, and more.

Tools and Costs

Function	Free Option	Paid Option (Best Value)
Invoicing	Wave	QuickBooks (£12/mo)
Scheduling	Calendly Free	Calendly Pro (£8/user/mo)
Data Entry	Google Forms	Docuf.AI (£20/mo)
CRM Automation	HubSpot Free	Salesforce Starter (£20/mo)
Workflow Agent	n8n Community	n8n Pro (€50/mo, ~£43/mo)

2. Quality Control: Consistency at Scale

Quality lapses can erode customer trust and profitability. AI-driven quality control—once only feasible for large manufacturers is now accessible to SMEs via cloud-based and smartphone-integrated solutions.

What Is It?

AI-powered quality control uses machine learning and computer vision to monitor, inspect, and flag issues in products or processes. This is increasingly accessible even for SMEs, thanks to cloud-based tools and smartphone integrations.

Practical Applications

- Manufacturing: Computer vision tools inspect products for defects, ensuring only high-quality goods reach customers.

- Service Consistency: AI analyses customer feedback and service delivery data to spot patterns and flag inconsistencies.
- Document Accuracy: AI-based proofreading (Grammarly, ChatGPT) ensures client-facing documents are error-free.

Pragmatic Actions:

- Identify Critical Quality Points: Pinpoint steps in your workflow where errors or inconsistencies most impact customers or costs.
- Deploy AI Tools: Start with document QC (Grammarly, ChatGPT) or basic image inspection using smartphone cameras and cloud AI services.
- Integrate Feedback Loops: Use AI to analyse customer feedback and flag recurring issues, then adjust processes accordingly.
- Scale Gradually: As confidence grows, explore more advanced computer vision or machine learning tools for physical product inspection.

Real-World Example:
A fashion SME deployed an AI chatbot to handle customer queries and order management, reducing customer service calls by 40% and boosting satisfaction by 25%.

Tools and Costs

Function	Free Option	Paid Option (Best Value)
Document QC	Grammarly Free	Grammarly Business (£12/mo)
Image Inspection	Google Photos AI	Custom CV tools (£50–£200/mo)
Feedback Analysis	Google Forms	Levity AI (£20/mo)

3. Predictive Maintenance: Preventing Downtime

Unplanned downtime is a major cost driver in manufacturing and logistics. Predictive maintenance leverages AI and IoT to turn reactive repairs into proactive asset management.

What Is It?

Predictive maintenance leverages AI and IoT sensors to monitor equipment in real time, predict failures, and schedule repairs before costly breakdowns occur. While this was once the domain of large manufacturers, affordable cloud-based solutions now put it within reach for SMEs.

Practical Applications

- Equipment Monitoring: AI analyses sensor data to detect wear, overheating, or abnormal vibrations, triggering alerts for preventive action.
- Maintenance Scheduling: AI tools optimise maintenance calendars, reducing unnecessary servicing and minimising downtime.
- Inventory Optimisation: By predicting part failures, SMEs can stock only what's needed, reducing inventory costs.

Pragmatic Actions:

- Start with Sensor Basics: Install affordable IoT sensors on critical equipment to collect data on usage, temperature, or vibration.
- Use Off-the-Shelf Analytics: Analyse sensor data with tools like Power BI or Microsoft 365 Copilot to spot patterns or anomalies.
- Automate Scheduling: Integrate AI insights with maintenance calendars to trigger service before failures occur.
- Review ROI Regularly: Compare downtime, maintenance costs, and equipment lifespan before and after implementation to quantify value.

Real-World Example:
Rubix, a UK manufacturing SME, used AI-powered predictive maintenance to cut unplanned downtime by 40% and save 25% in annual maintenance costs.

4. Data-Driven Decision-Making: Unlocking Operational Insights

Background:
Moving from intuition to data-driven operations is transformative for SMEs. AI can turn raw operational data into actionable insights for continuous improvement.

Pragmatic Actions:

- Centralise Data Collection: Use automation tools (n8n, Zapier) to pull data from various sources into a single dashboard.
- Pilot Analytics Projects: Start with a simple KPI, such as order fulfilment time or inventory turnover, and use AI analytics to identify improvement opportunities.
- Empower Teams: Train staff to interpret AI-generated insights and act on them, fostering a culture of continuous improvement.

Real-World Example:
A Viennese SME used AI analytics to become fully data-driven, uncovering hidden inefficiencies and improving decision-making speed and accuracy.

Consulting Tip: The "Automate, Optimize, Predict" Model

When evaluating operational AI opportunities, apply this three-step consulting model:

1. Automate the most repetitive, rules-based tasks.

2. Optimise processes for quality and consistency using AI analytics.
3. Predict future issues (downtime, demand spikes) with machine learning and real-time data.

This phased approach ensures quick wins, builds internal capability, and lays the foundation for advanced AI applications as your SME matures.

Tools and Costs

Function	Free Option	Paid Option (Best Value)
Sensor Data Analysis	Google Sheets	Microsoft 365 Copilot (£24/mo)
Maintenance Scheduling	Trello Free	UpKeep (£30/user/mo)
Predictive Analytics	Power BI Free	Power BI Pro (£10/user/mo)

Making AI Work in Your Operations: Practical Steps

1. Start with a Pain Point: Identify a repetitive or error-prone process—admin, inventory, quality checks, or maintenance.
2. Choose Off-the-Shelf Tools: Begin with free trials or basic plans from reputable providers; avoid custom builds unless absolutely necessary.
3. Integrate Gradually: Connect new AI tools to your existing workflows using automation platforms (e.g., n8n, Zapier, Microsoft Power Automate).
4. Measure and Iterate: Track time saved, error rates, and customer feedback. Use these metrics to justify further investment or expansion.

5. **Empower Your Team:** Involve staff in tool selection and training. Address concerns about job changes by emphasising how AI frees them for higher-value work.

Case Study 1: Micro Business (Under 10 Staff) (illustrative)

Company: Fresh Grounds Independent Coffee Shop (6 employees, Glasgow)

Challenge:
The owner and two staff spent hours each week managing supplier orders, tracking inventory, and responding to customer emails, leaving little time for customer engagement and new product development.

AI Solutions Implemented:

- Inventory Automation: QuickBooks AI (from £12/month) tracked ingredient usage and automatically reordered supplies when stocks ran low.
- Customer Communication: ChatGPT Plus (£16/month) drafted responses to common customer queries and managed online review replies.
- Scheduling: Calendly Free automated staff shift scheduling and meeting bookings.

Results (6 months):

- 10+ hours/week saved on admin and ordering.
- 50% reduction in stockouts and over-ordering.
- Customer review response time cut from days to hours.
- Owner freed up to launch two new menu items, driving a 12% sales increase.

Takeaway:
With a handful of affordable, easy-to-integrate AI tools, Fresh Grounds streamlined its "engine room", reduced waste, and improved customer service without hiring extra staff or investing in complex systems.

Case Study 2: Medium Enterprise (Under 200 Staff) (illustrative)

Company: TechFab Manufacturing – Precision Components Producer (145 employees, Midlands)

Challenge:
Manual quality inspections led to inconsistent product quality and occasional costly recalls. Equipment breakdowns caused unpredictable downtime, impacting delivery schedules and customer confidence.

AI Solutions Implemented:

- Quality Control: Integrated a cloud-based computer vision system (customised, £150/month) to inspect components for defects using standard webcams and AI models.
- Predictive Maintenance: Deployed Microsoft 365 Copilot (£24/user/month) to analyse IoT sensor data from key machines, predicting failures before they occurred.
- Process Automation with n8n: Implemented n8n Pro (€50/month, ~£43/month) to automate data flows between production, maintenance, and reporting systems, enabling seamless ticket creation, real-time alerts, and dashboard updates.
- Workflow Integration: Used n8n to connect quality control outputs with inventory management, ensuring defective batches were flagged and quarantined automatically.

Results (12 months):

- 30% reduction in defective products reaching customers.
- 22% decrease in unplanned equipment downtime.
- £80,000 annual savings from reduced recalls, improved uptime, and streamlined reporting.
- Enhanced customer satisfaction and retention, with on-time delivery rates up by 15%.

Takeaway:
By layering affordable AI solutions onto existing infrastructure and leveraging n8n as a flexible automation agent, TechFab Manufacturing achieved enterprise-level operational control and reliability—without the need for a large IT department or custom software builds.

Conclusion

AI-driven automation, quality control, and predictive maintenance are no longer futuristic ambitions; they are essential, accessible strategies for SMEs to compete, grow, and delight customers. By focusing on practical tools like n8n for medium enterprises and incremental improvements, SMEs can transform their operational "engine rooms" into engines of innovation, resilience, and profitability. Start small, learn fast, and let AI power your next leap forward.

Key Resources for SMEs:

- QuickBooks AI: Automated accounting and inventory, from £12/month.
- ChatGPT Plus: Customer communication and admin, £16/month.
- Calendly: Scheduling automation, free and paid plans.
- Microsoft 365 Copilot: Predictive analytics and maintenance, £24/user/month.

- n8n: Workflow automation for medium enterprises, Community Edition free/self-hosted, Pro from €50/month (~£43/month), and Enterprise custom pricing.
- Zapier: Workflow automation, free and paid plans.
- Custom Computer Vision: Quality control, from £50 to £200/month.

By leveraging these tools, even the smallest businesses can automate their engine rooms and unlock new levels of efficiency and growth.

CHAPTER 8

Marketing and Sales AI - From Leads to Loyalty

Customer Segmentation, Personalisation, Sales Forecasting, and Retention Strategies

Artificial intelligence is transforming the marketing and sales landscape for small and medium enterprises (SMEs). No longer reserved for global giants, AI now offers SMEs affordable, practical tools to attract leads, personalise campaigns, forecast sales, and build lasting customer loyalty. In this chapter, we'll explore how AI can supercharge your marketing and sales from the first touchpoint to lifelong retention using tools and strategies tailored to SME realities.

The Democratization of AI in Marketing and Sales

Until recently, AI-powered marketing and sales were the exclusive domain of large enterprises with big budgets and dedicated data teams. Today, cloud-based platforms and SaaS tools have made advanced AI accessible to SMEs, allowing even the smallest businesses to compete on personalisation, precision, and efficiency. According to recent studies, over 60% of SMEs using AI in marketing report improved lead quality, higher conversion rates, and increased customer retention, all at a fraction of the cost of traditional campaigns.

Why This Matters:
AI enables SMEs to move from "spray and pray" marketing to data-driven, targeted engagement. By automating segmentation, personalisation, and forecasting, SMEs can deliver the right message to the right customer at the right time, building loyalty and maximising ROI.

The Four Pillars of AI-Powered Marketing and Sales

1. Customer Segmentation: Targeting the Right Audience

Manual segmentation is time-consuming and often based on guesswork. AI automates this process, identifying micro-segments and behavioural patterns that humans might miss.

AI excels at analysing vast datasets to unearth hidden patterns and segments within your customer base. By leveraging these insights, SMEs can:

- Identify high-value customer segments based on behaviour, demographics, and engagement.
- Tailor messaging and offers to specific groups, increasing relevance and conversion rates.
- Automate segmentation in real time as new data comes in.

Tools:

- HubSpot CRM (Free & Paid): AI-driven segmentation and lead scoring.
- Zoho CRM (Free & Paid): Automatic clustering and tagging of customer groups.
- ActiveCampaign (from £19/month): behaviour-based segmentation for email and SMS campaigns.

Pragmatic Actions:

- Audit Your Data: Start by consolidating customer data from all sources (website, CRM, email, POS). Even basic info—purchase history, location, engagement—can be powerful when analysed by AI.
- Start with Built-In CRM Features: Use AI segmentation tools within your existing CRM (e.g., HubSpot, Zoho) to create dynamic lists based on real-time behaviour.
- Test and Refine: Run A/B tests on segmented groups to see which messages and offers resonate most.
- Automate Updates: Set up your CRM to automatically update segments as customers interact with your business.

Case Example: (illustrative)
A logistics SME used AI-driven segmentation to predict seasonal demand and adjust inventory, resulting in a 30% reduction in excess stock and a 20% drop in storage costs.

2. Personalisation: Creating One-to-One Experiences

Customers now expect brands to "know" them. AI enables SMEs to deliver Amazon-level personalisation without enterprise resources.

Personalisation is no longer a "nice-to-have"; it's a competitive necessity. AI enables SMEs to:

- Dynamically personalise email content, website experiences, and product recommendations.
- Use chatbots to provide tailored responses and offers 24/7.
- Optimise ad targeting based on real-time customer data.

Tools:

- Jasper AI (from £39/month): Generates personalised marketing copy and product descriptions.

- Klaviyo (Free & Paid): Personalises email and SMS campaigns based on customer actions.
- ManyChat (Free & Paid): Builds AI chatbots for Facebook Messenger and Instagram.

Pragmatic Actions:

- Deploy AI-Powered Email Tools: Use platforms like Klaviyo or ActiveCampaign to personalise subject lines, content, and send times based on user behaviour.
- Implement Chatbots: Start with a free or low-cost chatbot (ManyChat, Tidio) to provide personalised responses and collect lead data 24/7.
- Personalise Web Experiences: Use AI-driven website plugins that recommend products or content based on browsing history.
- Leverage Generative AI: Tools like Jasper can create unique, tailored copy for different customer personas in seconds.

Case Example: (illustrative)
A fashion SME integrated an AI chatbot for customer service and personalised recommendations, reducing customer service calls by 40% and boosting satisfaction by 25%. (https://www.activdev.com/en/artificial-intelligence-for-smes-case-studies-examples/)

3. Sales Forecasting: Predicting and Prioritizing Opportunities

Traditional sales forecasting relies on gut feel or static spreadsheets. AI uses real-time data, market trends, and customer signals for more accurate predictions.

AI-powered forecasting tools analyse historical sales data, market trends, and customer signals to:

- Predict which leads are most likely to convert, enabling focused sales efforts.

- Forecast revenue and identify potential pipeline gaps before they impact results.
- Recommend next-best actions for each sales opportunity.

Tools:

- Pipedrive (from £14.90/month): AI Sales Assistant predicts deal win probability and suggests actions.
- Salesforce Einstein (Enterprise): Advanced predictive analytics and opportunity scoring.
- Zoho CRM: Built-in AI for deal forecasting and pipeline management.

Pragmatic Actions:

- Connect Sales Data Sources: Integrate your CRM, e-commerce, and marketing platforms to feed data into your AI forecasting tool.
- Set Clear Metrics: Define what you want to predict, monthly sales, lead conversion rates, or pipeline gaps.
- Review and Adjust: Use AI recommendations to prioritise leads and adjust sales tactics. Regularly compare forecasts to actuals and refine your models.
- Pilot with a Subset: Start with one product line or sales team before scaling AI forecasting across the business.

Case Example: (illustrative)
A small fashion company used predictive analytics to anticipate trends and adjust collections, resulting in a 30% sales increase in six months. (https://www.activdev.com/en/artificial-intelligence-for-smes-case-studies-examples/).

4. Retention Strategies: Turning Customers into Advocates

It's 5 to 7 times more expensive to acquire a new customer than to keep an existing one. AI helps SMEs proactively identify churn risks and automate retention campaigns.

Keeping existing customers is more cost-effective than acquiring new ones. AI helps SMEs:

- Monitor customer sentiment and identify at-risk accounts.
- Automate loyalty campaigns and upsell recommendations.
- Analyse churn patterns and proactively address issues.

Tools:

- Customer.io (from £30/month): Automates retention and upsell messaging.
- Sprout Social (from £79/month): Monitors social sentiment and flags negative trends.
- AdRoll (from £25/month): Runs AI-powered retargeting and loyalty ads.

Pragmatic Actions:

- Monitor Sentiment: Use tools like Sprout Social or Customer.io to analyse reviews, social mentions, and support tickets for signs of dissatisfaction.
- Automate Loyalty Campaigns: Set up AI-triggered emails or SMS messages to reward repeat customers or win back those at risk of leaving.
- Personalise Offers: Use AI to suggest upsells or exclusive deals based on past purchases and engagement.
- Track and Optimise: Monitor retention metrics (repeat purchase rate, churn rate) and refine campaigns based on AI insights.

Case Example: (illustrative)

A local restaurant used AI to analyse loyalty program data and send personalized offers, increasing repeat visits by 25% and identifying at-risk customers for targeted campaigns. (https://www.activdev.com/en/artificial-intelligence-for-smes-case-studies-examples/)

Practical Steps to Get Started

1. Map Your Funnel: Identify key touchpoints where AI can add value—lead capture, segmentation, personalisation, sales forecasting, and retention.
2. Choose the Right Tools: Start with affordable, SME-friendly platforms HubSpot, Pipedrive, Jasper, Customer.io, n8n, and Sprout Social are all proven options.
3. Pilot and Measure: Launch a focused pilot (e.g., AI-powered email segmentation or chatbot for lead capture), track results, and iterate.
4. Integrate and Automate: Use workflow tools like n8n to connect your CRM, marketing, and sales platforms, ensuring data flows seamlessly and actions are triggered automatically.
5. Upskill Your Team: Provide basic AI and data literacy training. Encourage experimentation and share quick wins to build buy-in.
6. Monitor and Optimise: Regularly review campaign performance, customer feedback, and sales data. Use AI insights to refine targeting, messaging, and retention efforts.

Case Study 1: Micro Business (Under 10 Staff) (illustrative)

Company: "EcoGlow Candles", Artisan Candle Maker (7 employees, Bristol)

Challenge:
EcoGlow's founder struggled to identify which customers were most likely to buy again and wasted hours manually segmenting email lists. Social media engagement was sporadic, and email open rates lagged behind competitors.

AI Solutions Implemented:

- Customer Segmentation: Used HubSpot CRM (Free) to automatically segment customers by purchase history and engagement.
- Personalisation: Implemented Jasper AI (£39/month) to generate unique, personalised product recommendations and email content for each segment.
- Sales Forecasting: Leveraged Pipedrive's AI Sales Assistant (trial, then £14.90/month) to prioritise follow-ups with high-value leads.
- Retention: Automated post-purchase follow-ups and review requests using Customer.io (from £30/month).

Results (6 months):

- Email open rates increased from 17% to 29%; click-through rates doubled.
- The repeat purchase rate improved by 23%.
- Social engagement is up 40% through personalised content and chatbot responses.
- The owner saved 10+ hours per month on manual marketing tasks.

Takeaway:
By adopting affordable, user-friendly AI tools, EcoGlow Candles transformed their marketing from scattergun to strategic boosting, both efficiency and customer loyalty.

Case Study 2: Medium Enterprise (Under 200 Staff) (illustrative)

Company: "Urban Wheels" E-Bike Retailer & Service (120 employees, Manchester)

Challenge:
Urban Wheels faced inconsistent sales forecasting, high customer churn, and a lack of personalisation in marketing campaigns. Their sales and marketing teams operated in silos, missing cross-sell and upsell opportunities.

AI Solutions Implemented:

- Customer Segmentation & Personalisation: Deployed Salesforce Marketing Cloud (from £320/month) for advanced segmentation and personalised, automated campaigns across email, SMS, and social.
- Sales Forecasting: Integrated Salesforce Einstein for predictive analytics and pipeline management, enabling sales teams to focus on high-probability deals.
- Retention: Used Sprout Social (£79/month) to monitor social sentiment and respond to customer feedback in real time. Implemented AdRoll (£25/month) for AI-driven retargeting and loyalty campaigns.
- Workflow Automation: Leveraged n8n (Pro, €50/month) to connect marketing, sales, and service platforms—automating lead handoffs, customer onboarding, and feedback loops.

Results (12 months):

- Forecast accuracy improved by 27%, enabling better inventory and staffing decisions.
- Customer churn dropped by 18% as at-risk accounts were proactively engaged.

- Revenue per customer increased by 22% through targeted upsell and cross-sell campaigns.
- Marketing and sales teams reported a 30% productivity boost, with less time spent on manual data entry and more on strategic initiatives.

Takeaway:
Urban Wheels' integrated, AI-powered approach broke down departmental silos, delivering end-to-end visibility and a seamless customer journey from first touch to loyal advocate.

Conclusion

AI is now a business necessity for SMEs aiming to drive smarter marketing, more effective sales, and deeper customer loyalty. By focusing on segmentation, personalisation, forecasting, and retention—and leveraging affordable, off-the-shelf tools—SMEs can punch above their weight, delight customers, and fuel sustainable growth. The journey from leads to loyalty is no longer manual or guesswork-driven; with AI, it's measurable, scalable, and within reach for every ambitious business.

Key Tools for SME Marketing & Sales (Cost-Optimised):

Function	Free Option	Paid Option (Best Value)
CRM & Segmentation	HubSpot Free	Pipedrive (£14.90/mo), Zoho
Content Creation	Canva, Jasper Trial	Jasper (£39/mo)
Email Marketing	Mailchimp Free	ActiveCampaign (£19/mo)

Social Automation	Buffer Free	Sprout Social (£79/mo)
Workflow Automation	n8n Community	n8n Pro (€50/mo, ~£43/mo)
Retargeting Ads	AdRoll Free	AdRoll (£25/mo)

With these tools and strategies, your SME can create a marketing and sales engine that's not just reactive but predictive and proactive—turning every lead into a loyal customer.

CHAPTER 9

HR and People AI

Talent optimisation, recruitment automation, Performance Insights, and Employee Engagement Tools

The world of human resources is undergoing a profound transformation. For small and medium enterprises (SMEs), AI is no longer a distant promise; it's an accessible, pragmatic lever for attracting talent, optimising performance, and building a culture where people thrive. As AI automates routine tasks and delivers actionable insights, HR teams can finally focus on what matters most: nurturing people and driving business growth.

This chapter explores how SMEs can harness AI for recruitment automation, performance management, and employee engagement supported by real-world case studies and a focus on affordable, off-the-shelf solutions.

The New HR Reality: Why AI Matters for SMEs

- AI adoption in HR is accelerating rapidly, with 65% of companies now using AI for hiring in 2025, compared to just 10% a few years ago. This shift is driven by the need for efficiency, cost savings, and better decision-making in a competitive talent market. For SMEs, AI is not just about automation—it's about levelling the playing field

with larger organisations. AI enables SMEs to make smarter, data-driven decisions, personalise the employee experience, and respond quickly to changing business needs.
- AI is also redefining traditional HR roles. Instead of spending time on repetitive administrative work, HR professionals can now focus on strategic initiatives such as organisational growth, culture-building, and employee engagement. The move from a role-centric to a skills-centric model powered by AI-driven skills intelligence means SMEs can more accurately map workforce capabilities, identify gaps, and plan targeted upskilling and reskilling programmes. This is crucial for future-proofing the business and retaining top talent.

1. Recruitment Automation: Faster, Fairer, Smarter Hiring

What Can AI Do?

AI-powered recruitment tools streamline the end-to-end hiring process:

- Job advert creation: AI drafts inclusive, compelling job ads.
- Candidate sourcing: Automated search and outreach to passive candidates.
- CV screening: AI ranks applicants based on skills, experience, and even predicted fit.
- Video interview analysis: Tools like HireVue use AI to assess verbal and nonverbal cues, helping shortlist candidates efficiently.
- Bias mitigation: Algorithms anonymise applications and use objective scoring to support fairer hiring.

Tools and Costs

Function	Free Option	Paid Option (Best Value)
Job Ad Writing	ChatGPT Free	Jasper AI (£39/mo)
CV Screening	Zoho People Free	BambooHR (£5–£8/user/mo)
Video Interviews	Google Meet	HireVue (custom, SME pricing)
Scheduling	Calendly Free	Recruitee (£109/mo, up to 10 users)
Workflow Automation	n8n Community	n8n Pro (€50/mo, ~£43/mo)

2. Performance Insights: Real-Time, Actionable Analytics

What Can AI Do?

AI-driven performance management moves beyond annual reviews:

- Continuous feedback: Platforms like BambooHR and Sembly AI automate pulse surveys and feedback requests.
- Goal tracking: Smart dashboards monitor progress on KPIs and objectives.
- Predictive analytics: AI highlights employees at risk of burnout or attrition, enabling proactive support.
- Personalised development: AI recommends training and career paths tailored to each employee's strengths and ambitions.

Tools and Costs

Function	Free Option	Paid Option (Best Value)
Feedback & Surveys	Google Forms	Sembly AI ($10–$20/mo)
Performance Tracking	Zoho People Free	BambooHR (£5–£8/user/mo)
Analytics & Insights	Excel/Sheets	Microsoft 365 Copilot (£24/user/mo)
Learning Recommendations	Coursera Free	Leena AI (custom, SME pricing)

3. Employee Engagement: Building a Thriving Culture

What Can AI Do?

AI-powered employee engagement tools help SMEs:

- Monitor sentiment: Real-time analysis of survey responses, chat data, and even meeting transcripts.
- Automate HR helpdesk: Chatbots like Leena AI answer policy questions, handle leave requests, and onboard new hires.
- Personalise recognition: AI suggests timely, meaningful recognition for achievements.
- Benchmark culture: Compare engagement and retention metrics against industry standards.

Tools and Costs

Function	Free Option	Paid Option (Best Value)
Engagement Surveys	Google Forms	Leena AI (custom)
HR Chatbot	ChatGPT Free	Leena AI (custom)
Sentiment Analysis	Sembly AI Free	Sembly AI Team ($20/mo)

Pragmatic Actions for SMEs: Getting Started with AI in HR

- Map Your HR Processes: Start by mapping out your current HR workflows, identifying repetitive tasks, and pinpointing where delays or errors occur (such as manual CV screening, slow onboarding, or inconsistent feedback cycles). This will help you prioritise where AI can deliver the most immediate value.
- Start Small and Scale: Pilot AI in a single HR function, such as automating candidate screening or deploying a chatbot for employee queries. Use free or low-cost tools (e.g., Zoho People, ChatGPT, Google Forms) to minimise risk and investment at the outset. Measure the time saved, quality of hires, or employee satisfaction, and use these metrics to build the case for broader adoption.
- Leverage Skills Intelligence: Use AI platforms to assess your workforce's current skills and identify gaps relative to your business goals. This enables targeted training, supports internal mobility, and helps you plan for future talent needs. Personalised learning plans and just-in-time training recommendations can be delivered using AI-powered tools, boosting engagement and retention.
- Automate Compliance and Data Management: AI can help SMEs stay compliant by tracking regulatory updates, automating report

generation (e.g., for tax, EEO, or DEI), and managing sensitive employee data more efficiently and securely. This reduces legal risk and administrative overhead.

- Enhance Onboarding and Engagement: Implement AI-driven onboarding assistants to guide new hires through their first days, connect them with mentors, and recommend relevant training resources. Real-time sentiment analysis tools can monitor employee engagement, flagging issues before they escalate and enabling proactive interventions.
- Integrate and Connect Systems: Use workflow automation tools (like n8n) to connect disparate HR, payroll, and scheduling systems, reducing manual data entry and minimising errors. This integration creates a seamless HR ecosystem, freeing up HR staff for higher-value tasks.
- Maintain the Human Element: While AI can automate and optimise many HR functions, SMEs should ensure that critical touchpoints such as interviews, conflict resolution, and sensitive feedback remain human-led. AI should augment, not replace, the personal relationships that are central to a healthy workplace.
- Monitor, Learn, and Iterate: Regularly review the impact of AI tools, gather feedback from users, and refine your approach. As confidence and familiarity grow, expand automation to additional HR processes and explore more advanced AI capabilities (such as predictive analytics for attrition or performance management).

By taking these pragmatic steps, SMEs can harness AI to optimise talent management, drive business growth, and create a more agile, engaged workforce without the need for large budgets or complex IT infrastructure.

Case Study 1: Micro Business (Under 10 Staff) (illustrative)

Company: "GreenTech Solutions" – Environmental Consultancy (8 employees, Leeds)

Challenge:
The founder spent hours every week on manual recruitment—writing job ads, screening CVs, and scheduling interviews. Employee feedback was informal and inconsistent, making it hard to spot issues early.

AI Solutions Implemented:

- Recruitment Automation: Used Zoho People (Free) to automate job postings, CV screening, and interview scheduling.
- Job Ad Writing: Leveraged ChatGPT Free to draft inclusive, engaging adverts.
- Performance Insights: Adopted Sembly AI (Personal, Free; later Team, $20/mo) for automated meeting summaries and sentiment tracking.
- Engagement: Monthly pulse surveys via Google Forms, with Sembly AI analysing results for trends.

Results (6 months):

- Time-to-hire reduced by 50%; hiring costs down by 60%.
- The founder saved 6+ hours/week on admin.
- Employee satisfaction scores improved by 18% with early detection of burnout risks.
- More structured feedback led to a 25% improvement in project delivery times.

Takeaway:
With free and low-cost AI tools, GreenTech Solutions professionalised its HR processes, improved team engagement, and freed up leadership to focus on growth.

Case Study 2: Medium Enterprise (Under 200 Staff) (illustrative)

Company: "Nova Retail Group" – Specialty Retailer (140 employees, Birmingham)

Challenge:
Rapid growth led to inconsistent hiring, high turnover in key roles, and lack of real-time insight into employee engagement and performance.

AI Solutions Implemented:

- Recruitment Automation: Implemented BambooHR (£5–£8/user/mo) for automated applicant tracking, onboarding, and performance management.
- Video Interviewing: Integrated HireVue (custom SME pricing) for AI-powered video screening, reducing bias and improving candidate fit.
- Performance Insights: Used Microsoft 365 Copilot (£24/user/mo) to analyse performance data and predict attrition risks.
- Employee Engagement: Rolled out Leena AI for automated HR helpdesk, onboarding, and pulse surveys, with sentiment analytics.
- Workflow Automation: Deployed n8n Pro (€50/mo, ~£43/mo) to connect HR, payroll, and scheduling systems, reducing manual re-entry and errors.

Results (12 months):

- Average time-to-hire dropped by 38%; recruitment costs are down by 44%.
- Turnover in key roles reduced by 21% through early intervention and tailored development.
- Employee engagement scores are up 27%; absenteeism is down 15%.
- The HR team saved 30+ hours/month on admin; managers received real-time performance insights.

Takeaway:

By layering affordable AI solutions across the employee lifecycle and integrating workflows with n8n, Nova Retail Group built a scalable, data-driven HR function—delivering measurable gains in retention, engagement, and operational efficiency.

Conclusion

AI is now an essential part of the SME HR toolkit, enabling faster recruitment, smarter performance management, and stronger employee engagement. By focusing on practical, affordable solutions and blending automation with human oversight, SMEs can build a people-first culture that drives business growth. Start small, measure impact, and let AI unlock the full potential of your team.

Key Tools for SME HR (Cost-Optimised):

Function	Free Option	Paid Option (Best Value)
Recruitment	Zoho People Free	BambooHR (£5–£8/user/mo)
Job Ad Writing	ChatGPT Free	Jasper AI (£39/mo)
Video Interviews	Google Meet	HireVue (custom)
Performance Tracking	Sembly AI Free	Sembly AI Team ($20/mo)
Engagement Surveys	Google Forms	Leena AI (custom)
Workflow Automation	n8n Community	n8n Pro (€50/mo, ~£43/mo)

With these tools and strategies, SMEs can modernise HR, optimise talent, and create workplaces where people and businesses thrive.

PART IV
IMPLEMENTATION

CHAPTER 10

Getting Started

Your First AI Project Choosing the Right Pilot, Setting Expectations, and Measuring Success

AI is rapidly becoming a differentiator for SMEs, offering the ability to automate routine work, uncover actionable insights, and compete with larger organisations without a heavy resource burden. However, the journey from AI interest to implementation can be daunting due to the abundance of tools, technical language, and uncertainty about ROI. A focused pilot project helps SMEs overcome these barriers by providing a manageable, low-risk way to build internal capability, demonstrate tangible value, and foster a culture of innovation. Pilots also allow SMEs to learn from small-scale experiments, reducing the risk of costly missteps when scaling up.

For small and medium-sized enterprises (SMEs), the leap from AI curiosity to real-world results begins with a single, well-chosen pilot project. This first step is critical: it builds confidence, demonstrates value, and lays the groundwork for broader adoption. Yet, many business leaders feel overwhelmed by the options, technical jargon, and uncertainty about where to begin. This chapter demystifies the process, offering a clear, pragmatic roadmap to select, launch, and measure your first AI project with real SME case studies and a focus on affordable, off-the-shelf solutions.

1. Choosing the Right Pilot: Where to Start

Identify High-Impact, Low-Risk Opportunities

For SMEs, the risk of resource waste or disruption is a real concern. A pilot project is a safe, controlled way to explore AI's potential while minimising business risk. Pilots allow you to learn, adapt, and build internal confidence before committing to larger investments. Many SMEs succeed by starting with "pain point mapping", identifying bottlenecks or repetitive tasks that drain time and morale.

Your first AI project should solve a real business pain point, offer measurable benefits, and be feasible given your resources. The sweet spot is a project that's important enough to matter but simple enough to deliver results within 3–6 months, long enough to see impact and short enough to maintain momentum and stakeholder interest.

Common pilot project areas for SMEs:

- Automating repetitive admin (invoicing, scheduling, data entry)
- Customer service chatbots to handle routine queries
- Sales or marketing analytics for campaign optimization
- Predictive maintenance in manufacturing or logistics

Key selection criteria:

- Clear business value (cost savings, time reduction, revenue boost)
- Data availability (even a modest amount of clean, relevant data)
- Minimal disruption to core operations
- Quick wins and visible outcomes

Pragmatic Actions:

- Pain Point Workshop: Run a short workshop with key staff to list and score daily pain points. Use sticky notes or digital boards to visualise where AI could help.
- Consulting Model: Consider a "Discovery Sprint" with an external consultant, typically a 2–4 week engagement, to help identify and prioritise the top 1–2 use cases for piloting.
- Quick Feasibility Check: For each candidate process, ask: Is the data available? Is the process well-defined? Is there a clear metric for improvement?

Tip: List routine tasks your team handles, then score them for impact and effort. Prioritise those with high impact and low to medium effort for your first AI pilot.

2. Setting Clear Objectives and Expectations

Define Success Upfront

Setting clear, measurable objectives is critical to avoid "pilot purgatory", where projects stall due to vague goals or moving targets. Aligning your pilot's aims with business outcomes ensures buy-in from leadership and staff alike. Realistic expectations help prevent disappointment and foster a learning mindset.

Before you select a tool or vendor, define what success looks like. Set specific, measurable objectives tied to business outcomes such as:

- "Reduce customer service response time by 50%."
- "Automate 30% of invoice processing."
- "Increase repeat sales by 15% in six months."

Break your pilot into clear phases with deadlines, and build in buffer time for unexpected challenges.

Prepare Your Data

AI runs on data. Identify what data your pilot will need and where it currently resides. Assess its quality: is it complete, accurate, and consistent? If there are gaps, set up processes to collect missing information—this might mean tweaking forms, updating spreadsheets, or integrating new data sources.

Pragmatic Actions:

- SMART Goals: Use the SMART framework (Specific, Measurable, Achievable, Relevant, Time-bound) to define pilot objectives.
- Stakeholder Alignment: Hold a kickoff meeting with all stakeholders to agree on success criteria and timelines.
- Consulting Model: Engage a consultant for an "Objective Setting Workshop" to facilitate consensus and document KPIs.
- Data Audit Checklist: Assign someone to review data sources for completeness and quality; create a simple checklist to track progress.

3. Selecting the Right AI Solution

Match Tools to Your Needs

The AI marketplace is vast and can be overwhelming. SMEs benefit from choosing off-the-shelf solutions designed for ease of use and rapid deployment. Integration with existing systems is often more important than advanced features.

Look for AI solutions that fit your pilot's goals, budget, and technical capacity. For most SMEs, off-the-shelf tools are ideal; they're affordable, require minimal setup, and integrate with existing systems.

Consider:

- Features and ease of use
- Integration with your current software stack
- Vendor support and training resources
- Pricing (free trials, pay-as-you-go, SME packages)

Popular SME-friendly tools:

- Customer service: ChatGPT Plus (£16/mo), Tidio (free/paid), Zoho Desk
- Process automation: Zapier (free/paid), n8n (Community free, Pro €50/mo), Microsoft Power Automate
- Finance: QuickBooks AI (£12/mo), Xero
- Sales/marketing: HubSpot CRM (free/paid), Jasper AI (£39/mo)

Pragmatic Actions:

- Vendor Demos: Schedule short demos with 2–3 vendors to compare usability and support.
- Trial Periods: Take advantage of free trials or pilot licences to test tools in your real environment.
- Consulting Model: Use a "Solution Matchmaking" service. Some consultants offer vendor-neutral advice and can shortlist the best-fit tools for your needs.
- Integration Plan: Map out how the new tool will connect with your existing software; involve IT or an external advisor early.

4. Planning and Implementing Your Pilot

Successful pilots depend on cross-functional collaboration. Even in small teams, involving the right people ensures smoother adoption and better results. A structured plan keeps the project on track and surfaces issues early.

Build the Right Team

Even a small pilot benefits from cross-functional collaboration. Involve:

- A project lead (often the business owner or a tech-savvy manager)
- Process owners (those closest to the workflow you're automating)
- IT support (internal or external, as needed)
- Vendor or consultant support (for setup/training, if required)

Create a Step-by-Step Plan

Break down the implementation into manageable tasks, such as:

- Data collection and preparation
- Tool selection and setup
- Integration with existing systems
- Staff training
- Testing and feedback loops

Pragmatic Actions:

- RACI Matrix: Create a simple RACI (Responsible, Accountable, Consulted, Informed) chart to clarify roles.
- Weekly Stand-Ups: Hold brief weekly check-ins to track progress, surface blockers, and celebrate small wins.
- Consulting Model: Consider a "Pilot Implementation Package" from a consultant, including setup, training, and troubleshooting support.
- Staff Training: Use vendor-provided tutorials or schedule a live Q&A to boost confidence and skills.

Tip: Use vendor-provided training and documentation to minimise learning curves and maximise adoption.

5. Measuring Success and Iterating

Continuous measurement and iteration are hallmarks of successful AI adoption. Pilots are learning opportunities; what matters most is capturing insights and refining your approach.

Monitor, Evaluate, and Adjust

Track your pilot's performance against the objectives you set. Key metrics might include:

- Time saved (hours/week)
- Cost reduction (£/month)
- Error rates or customer satisfaction scores
- Revenue impact or sales conversion rates

Gather feedback from users and customers. Be ready to tweak workflows, retrain staff, or adjust tool settings based on real-world results.

Pragmatic Actions:

- Dashboard: Set up a simple dashboard (Excel, Google Sheets, or built-in tool analytics) to track key metrics.
- Feedback Loop: Collect feedback from users at regular intervals—short surveys or informal interviews work well.
- Consulting Model: Engage a consultant for a "Pilot Review Session" to help analyse results and recommend next steps.
- Iteration Plan: Document what worked, what didn't, and propose adjustments for the next cycle.

Celebrate and Communicate Wins

Share early successes with your team and stakeholders. This builds momentum and buy-in for future AI projects.

6. Scaling Up: From Pilot to Broader Adoption

Scaling AI requires a deliberate, stepwise approach. Early wins build momentum, but it's important to consolidate learning and ensure readiness before expanding.

Once your pilot is delivering value, consider where else AI could help. Gradually scale up, applying lessons learnt and expanding to new processes or departments. Remember, successful AI adoption is iterative—start small, learn fast, and grow with confidence.

Practical Steps and Tips for Your First AI Project

1. Start with a business pain point: focus on a process that's repetitive, time-consuming, or error-prone.
2. Set clear, measurable goals: Define what success looks like before you start.
3. Choose affordable, easy-to-integrate tools: Prioritise solutions that work with your existing systems and don't require heavy IT investment.
4. Prepare your data: Ensure you have enough quality data for your chosen use case.
5. Engage your team: Involve those closest to the process and provide basic training.
6. Monitor, measure, and iterate: Track results and adjust as needed.
7. Scale up gradually: Use early wins to build momentum and expand AI adoption.

Pragmatic Actions:

- Lessons Learnt Workshop: Host a debrief with your pilot team to capture insights and update your AI roadmap.
- Internal Case Study: Document your pilot as a short case study to share with other teams and leadership.
- Consulting Model: Use a "Scale-Up Roadmap" service. Consultants can help plan phased rollouts and change management.
- Peer Learning: Join SME AI forums or local business networks to exchange lessons and avoid common pitfalls.

These additions provide both deeper context and actionable steps for SMEs, ensuring your chapter is both informative and practical for readers embarking on their first AI project.

Case Study 1: Micro Business (Under 10 Staff) (illustrative)

Company: "Bright Copy" – B2B Copywriting Agency (8 employees, London)

Challenge:
The team was bogged down by repetitive admin—scheduling, invoicing, and handling client queries—leaving less time for billable creative work.

Pilot Project:
Automate client communications and proposal drafting using ChatGPT Plus (£16/month) and Calendly AI Scheduler (£8/user/month).

Objectives:

- Cut proposal turnaround time by 50%
- Reduce admin hours by 30%
- Improve client response time

Implementation:

- Exported three months of client emails to train ChatGPT on tone and FAQs
- Integrated Calendly with team calendars for automated scheduling
- Provided a one-hour workshop for staff on using the new tools

Results (3 months):

- Proposal turnaround time reduced by 58%
- 10+ admin hours saved per week
- Client satisfaction scores up 20%
- The team reported less burnout and more time for creative work

Takeaway:
A focused, low-risk AI pilot delivered immediate, measurable benefits and set the stage for further automation.

Case Study 2: Medium Enterprise (Under 200 Staff) (illustrative)

Company: "Northfield Manufacturing" – Precision Engineering (160 employees, Midlands)

Challenge:
Manual production scheduling and reactive maintenance led to costly delays and excess inventory.

Pilot Project:
Implement predictive maintenance using Microsoft 365 Copilot (£24/user/month) and automate maintenance ticketing with n8n Pro (€50/month).

Objectives:

- Reduce unplanned equipment downtime by 20%
- Decrease inventory holding costs by 15%
- Improve on-time delivery rates

Implementation:

- Collected 12 months of sensor and maintenance log data
- Set up Microsoft Copilot to analyze patterns and predict failures
- Used n8n to automate ticket creation and alerting for maintenance teams
- Trained supervisors to interpret AI alerts and schedule repairs proactively

Results (6 months):

- 23% reduction in downtime
- 17% decrease in inventory costs
- £110,000 annual savings
- On-time delivery improved by 15%

Takeaway:
A targeted AI pilot in operations delivered substantial ROI, built internal confidence, and provided a template for scaling AI across other business functions.

Conclusion

Launching your first AI project doesn't have to be daunting. By starting small, focusing on real business needs, and choosing the right tools, SMEs can unlock immediate value and lay the foundation for broader AI-driven transformation. Remember: the most important step is the first one taken with clarity, confidence, and a commitment to learning and improvement.

Key Tools for Your First AI Project (SME-Friendly):

Function	Free Option	Paid Option (Best Value)
Customer Service	Tidio Free	ChatGPT Plus (£16/mo)
Scheduling	Calendly Free	Calendly AI (£8/user/mo)
Process Automation	Zapier Free	n8n Pro (€50/mo, ~£43/mo)
Finance	Wave Accounting	QuickBooks AI (£12/mo)
Operations	Google Sheets	Microsoft 365 Copilot (£24/user/mo)

By following this roadmap, your business can move from AI aspiration to real-world impact—one practical, measurable project at a time.

CHAPTER 11

Data Foundations

Getting Your House in Order Data Quality, Governance, and Integration Essentials for SMEs

For small and medium-sized enterprises (SMEs), the promise of AI-driven transformation hinges on one critical asset: data. Without robust data quality, clear governance, and effective integration, even the best AI tools will fail to deliver meaningful results. This chapter provides a practical, step-by-step guide to building strong data foundations, demystifying what's essential, how to get started, and which tools make sense for SMEs. Real-world case studies illustrate how businesses of all sizes can turn data from a liability into a strategic advantage.

Why Data Foundations Matter for SMEs

Data is the fuel for AI and analytics. But for many SMEs, data is scattered across spreadsheets, cloud apps, and legacy systems, often incomplete, inconsistent, or poorly secured. The risks are real: poor data quality leads to bad decisions. compliance headaches, and missed opportunities. Conversely, good data governance and integration unlock better insights, smoother operations, and a clear path to AI adoption.

1. Data Quality: The Bedrock of Reliable Insights

By 2025, 78% of SMEs cite poor data quality as their top barrier to AI adoption. High-quality data isn't just about accuracy; it's the foundation for predictive analytics, personalised customer experiences, and automated workflows. SMEs that prioritise data quality see 30% faster decision-making and 25% fewer operational errors.

What Is Data Quality?

Data quality refers to the accuracy, completeness, consistency, and reliability of your data assets. High-quality data is fit for purpose: it reflects reality, supports business decisions, and is trusted by users.

Why It Matters

- Accurate analysis: Decisions based on bad data can be costly.
- Operational efficiency: Clean data reduces errors and rework.
- Regulatory compliance: Inaccurate or missing data can lead to legal and financial penalties.

How to Improve Data Quality

- Assess your current state: Audit your key data assets, customer lists, sales records, inventory, and HR files, and identify gaps or inconsistencies.
- Define data quality rules: Set clear standards for data entry, formats, and required fields. For example, require valid email formats or complete addresses.
- Clean and validate: Regularly remove duplicates, correct errors, and fill in missing information. Use data validation tools or features built into your CRM, accounting, or HR software.

- Monitor continuously: Implement data quality dashboards or periodic audits to catch issues early.

Tools for SMEs:

- Google Sheets/Excel: Built-in data validation and cleaning functions (free/low cost).
- Zoho CRM/QuickBooks: Automated data checks and deduplication (from £12/month).
- OpenRefine: Free, open-source tool for cleaning messy data.

Practical Steps for SMEs: Building Data Foundations

1. Audit your data: Identify key data assets, where they live, and their current quality.
2. Set clear data policies: Document how data should be collected, stored, and shared. Assign ownership.
3. Clean and validate: Use simple tools to fix errors and standardise formats. Set up regular checks.
4. Automate integration: Connect systems with tools like Zapier or n8n to reduce manual work and errors.
5. Educate and empower: Train your team on data best practices and the importance of governance.
6. Monitor and improve: Use dashboards and audits to track data quality and compliance. Update policies as your business evolves.

2. Data Governance: Setting the Rules and Roles

What Is Data Governance?

40% of SME data breaches stem from poor access controls and undocumented policies. Robust governance reduces compliance risks and builds stakeholder trust—critical for AI initiatives requiring sensitive data.

Data governance is the framework of policies, procedures, and standards that dictate how data is collected, stored, accessed, and used within your business. Think of it as your company's "data rulebook".

Why It Matters

- Trust and accountability: Everyone knows who owns which data and how it should be handled.
- Security and privacy: Protects sensitive information from breaches and ensures compliance with laws like GDPR.
- Consistency and clarity: Reduces confusion and errors, especially as your business grows.

How to Implement Data Governance

- Define clear data policies: Document how data is collected, stored, interpreted, and shared. Include data ownership, access controls, and security measures.
- Establish data standards: Set guidelines for data entry, naming conventions, and formats to ensure consistency.
- Assign data ownership: Designate responsible individuals (data owners/stewards) for key datasets. This fosters a culture of responsibility and improves quality.
- Implement security measures: Use encryption, access controls, and regular backups. Adhere to GDPR and other relevant regulations.
- Monitor and audit: Regularly review data quality, compliance, and security. Update policies as your business evolves or regulations change.
- Educate your team: Train employees on data governance policies and best practices, including data privacy and security awareness.

Pragmatic Actions:

- Assign Data Stewards: Designate 1–2 employees per department to oversee data entry, quality, and access. Provide basic training on GDPR principles.
- Create a "Data Rulebook": Draft a 5-page policy covering data ownership, retention periods, and breach protocols. Use templates from Intalio or Microsoft Compliance Manager.
- Conduct Quarterly Compliance Drills: Simulate data access requests or breaches to test response times and update protocols.
- Consulting Model: Hire a fractional Data Protection Officer (DPO) for 4–8 hours/month to audit practices and prepare for regulatory inspections.

Tools for SMEs:

- Intalio Data Governance Toolkit: Affordable, SME-focused platform for managing policies, ownership, and compliance.
- Microsoft 365: Built-in security, access controls, and compliance features (from £5/user/month).
- Google Workspace: Access management, sharing controls, and audit logs (from £4.60/user/month).

3. Data Integration: Unifying Your Information

SMEs using integrated data platforms report 50% faster reporting and 35% cost savings from reduced manual work. AI tools like chatbots or predictive analytics require real-time data flows across CRM, ERP, and marketing systems.

What Is Data Integration?

Data integration is the process of connecting data from different sources – spreadsheets, cloud apps, and databases so it can be used together for reporting, analytics, or AI.

Why It Matters

- Single source of truth: Reduces errors and duplicated effort.
- Faster insights: Enables real-time dashboards and automated workflows.
- AI readiness: Most AI tools require unified, accessible data to function effectively.

How to Achieve Effective Integration

- Map your data landscape: List all the places where key business data lives (CRM, accounting, HR, e-commerce, spreadsheets).
- Automate connections: Use workflow automation tools (like Zapier or n8n) to sync data between systems, reducing manual re-entry and errors.
- Centralise where possible: consider moving to cloud-based platforms that integrate multiple functions (e.g., Zoho One, Microsoft 365).
- Monitor data flows: Set up alerts or dashboards to track data movement and spot integration failures quickly.

Pragmatic Actions:

- Map Data Flows with Lucidchart: Visualise how data moves between tools (e.g., Shopify → QuickBooks → email lists). Identify bottlenecks like manual CSV exports.

- Automate with SME-Friendly Tools: Use n8n to connect APIs (e.g., sync HubSpot contacts with Mailchimp) or Zapier for simple app workflows.
- Adopt a "Platform-First" Approach: Migrate to all-in-one suites like Zoho One (£25/user/month) to minimise integration complexity.
- Consulting Model: Partner with an integration specialist for a "2-Day Connector Sprint" to automate 3–5 critical workflows using existing tools.

Tools for SMEs:

- Zapier: Easy, no-code automation between 5,000+ apps (free/paid, from £20/month).
- n8n: Open-source workflow automation for more complex integrations (Community free, Pro €50/month).
- Microsoft Power Automate: Integrates with the Microsoft ecosystem and many third-party apps (from £12.40/user/month).

Pragmatic Actions:

- Run a "Data Health Check" Workshop: Audit 3–5 critical datasets (e.g., customer records, inventory) using free tools like Excel's Data Profiling or OpenRefine. Score each dataset for completeness, accuracy, and consistency.
- Implement Automated Validation: Use Zoho CRM or Google Sheets to set rules (e.g., mandatory fields, email format checks) that block invalid entries at the source.
- Adopt Master Data Management (MDM): For SMEs with siloed data, use lightweight MDM tools like Pimcore (open-source) to create a single customer/product view.
- Consulting Model: Engage a data consultant for a "Fix-It Fortnight"—a two-week sprint to clean priority datasets and train staff on maintenance.

Case Study 1: Micro Business (Under 10 Staff) (illustrative)

Company: "EcoGlow Candles" – Artisan Candle Maker (7 employees, Bristol)

Challenge:
EcoGlow's data was scattered across spreadsheets, email, and their e-commerce platform. Customer lists were riddled with duplicates and missing information, leading to failed deliveries and marketing misfires.

Solution:

- Data Quality: Used Google Sheets' data validation and OpenRefine (free) to clean and standardise customer data.
- Governance: The owner created simple data entry rules and assigned one team member as "data steward" for customer information.
- Integration: Connected their e-commerce platform and email marketing tool using Zapier (free tier), ensuring new orders and contacts were automatically synced and deduplicated.

Results (6 months):

- Customer data accuracy improved from 70% to 98%.
- Marketing email bounce rates dropped by 40%.
- Fewer delivery errors and increased repeat purchases.
- The team spent 60% less time on manual data fixes.

Takeaway:
With basic tools and clear policies, EcoGlow built a strong data foundation—unlocking better marketing, smoother operations, and happier customers.

Case Study 2: Medium Enterprise (Under 200 Staff) (illustrative)

Company: "Nova Retail Group" – Specialty Retailer (140 employees, Birmingham)

Challenge:
Rapid growth left Nova with siloed data across sales, inventory, HR, and finance. Inconsistent formats and lack of ownership led to reporting errors and compliance risks.

Solution:

- Data Quality: Implemented Zoho CRM and QuickBooks, using built-in data validation and deduplication features.
- Governance: Adopted Intalio Data Governance Toolkit (pricing scaled for SMEs) to document policies, assign data owners, and monitor compliance.
- Integration: Deployed n8n Pro (€50/month) to automate data flows between sales, inventory, and HR systems, creating unified dashboards and real-time alerts.
- Training: Ran quarterly data governance workshops for all staff, building a culture of accountability and awareness.

Results (12 months):

- Reporting errors reduced by 75%.
- Real-time, integrated dashboards enabled faster decision-making.
- Passed the GDPR compliance audit with no major findings.
- Data-related support tickets dropped by 60%.

Takeaway:
By investing in data governance, quality, and integration, Nova Retail Group turned data chaos into a strategic asset—supporting compliance, efficiency, and growth.

Conclusion

Strong data foundations are the bedrock of AI success for SMEs. By focusing on quality, governance, and integration with clear policies, responsible ownership, and the right tools, businesses of any size can unlock the full value of their information. Start simple, build incrementally, and let your data become a source of insight, efficiency, and competitive advantage.

Key Tools for SME Data Foundations:

Function	Free Option	Paid Option (Best Value)
Data Cleaning	OpenRefine, Sheets	Zoho CRM, QuickBooks (£12/mo)
Governance	Manual docs	Intalio Toolkit (SME pricing)
Integration	Zapier Free	n8n Pro (€50/mo, ~£43/mo)
Security	Google Workspace	Microsoft 365 (£5/user/mo)

With these essentials in place, your SME will be ready to harness AI and data-driven decision-making with confidence and clarity.

CHAPTER 12

Technology Choices - Build, Buy, or Partner:

Navigating Vendors, Platforms, and Implementation Approaches

For small and medium-sized enterprises (SMEs), the decision of how to bring AI into your business is as important as the technology itself. The right approach can accelerate growth, streamline operations, and create a competitive advantage. The wrong one can drain resources, stall momentum, and leave you locked into tools that don't fit your needs. This chapter demystifies the "build, buy, or partner" decision, offering a practical framework, real-world case studies, and guidance on how to choose the best path for your business.

The Three Paths to AI Implementation

AI adoption for SMEs generally falls into three categories: build, buy, or partner. Each comes with distinct advantages, risks, and ideal use cases. Increasingly, hybrid "buy-to-build" models are emerging, blending the best of both worlds.

1. Build: Develop In-House AI Solutions

Building in-house AI solutions is often seen as the most ambitious path, but it can also be the most rewarding for SMEs with unique processes or intellectual property. However, this approach requires a clear-eyed assessment of internal capabilities, as the shortage of AI talent and the complexity of ongoing maintenance can strain smaller teams. For many SMEs, the decision to build is driven by regulatory requirements, niche industry needs, or a desire to own and control sensitive data and algorithms.

What it means:
You assemble your own team of data scientists, engineers, and domain experts to create custom AI tailored to your business's unique needs.

When to choose it:

- You have highly specific requirements not met by existing products.
- AI is core to your competitive advantage or business model.
- You have (or can access) the technical talent and resources to support ongoing development and maintenance.

Pros:

- Maximum control over features, data, and intellectual property.
- Tailored to your exact processes and needs.

Cons:

- High upfront and ongoing costs (talent, infrastructure, maintenance).
- Longer time to market.
- Risk of technical debt and "Frankenstack" architectures if not managed with discipline.
- Can distract from your core business unless AI is a strategic differentiator.

Pragmatic Actions:

- Capability Assessment: Conduct a skills and resource audit to determine if your team can realistically support end-to-end AI development.
- Proof-of-Concept First: Start with a narrow proof-of-concept (PoC) project to test feasibility and value before scaling up.
- Leverage Open Source: Use open-source AI frameworks (e.g., TensorFlow, PyTorch) to reduce costs and accelerate development.
- Consulting Model: Engage a fractional CTO or AI architect for a "Build Readiness Assessment", a short-term engagement to validate your approach, identify gaps, and recommend best practices.
- Plan for Maintenance: Allocate resources for ongoing monitoring, updates, and technical debt management to avoid future bottlenecks.

2. Buy: Off-the-Shelf AI Tools and Platforms

The SaaS revolution has democratised access to advanced AI, making it possible for SMEs to deploy sophisticated solutions without deep technical knowledge. Off-the-shelf tools are especially attractive for SMEs looking for rapid deployment, predictable costs, and minimal disruption. However, the trade-off is less flexibility and potential challenges integrating with legacy systems.

What it means:
You license or subscribe to existing AI-powered software, CRM, chatbots, analytics, and automation often delivered as SaaS.

When to choose it:

- Your needs are standard or similar to many other businesses.
- You want quick, cost-effective implementation.
- You lack in-house AI expertise or want to minimise risk.

Pros:

- Fast deployment, often in days or weeks.
- Lower upfront cost and predictable subscription fees.
- Access to vendor support, updates, and a broader user community.
- Benefit from continuous innovation and improvements.

Cons:

- Limited customisation.
- Potential integration challenges with legacy systems.
- Vendor lock-in and dependence on their roadmap.
- If competitors use the same tools, differentiation may be limited.

Pragmatic Actions:

- Needs Mapping: List all business processes that could benefit from AI and prioritise those with the highest impact and lowest complexity.
- Product Trials: Pilot at least two competing solutions to compare usability, integration, and support before committing.
- Integration Checklist: Ensure any tool under consideration offers open APIs or pre-built connectors for your existing systems (e.g., accounting, CRM).
- Consulting Model: Use a "Vendor Selection Sprint", a consultant-led, 2–4 week process to shortlist, demo, and score vendors against your requirements.
- Negotiate Flexibility: Seek month-to-month contracts or pilots to minimise risk and maintain leverage with vendors.

3. Partner: Collaborate with AI Specialists

Partnering with AI consultants or managed service providers allows SMEs to access top-tier expertise without the cost and risk of hiring full-time staff. This approach is ideal for complex, evolving needs or when customisation is required but internal capacity is limited. The success of this model relies on clear communication, shared goals, and well-defined deliverables.

What it means:
You work with a consultancy, systems integrator, or managed service provider to co-develop or tailor AI solutions.

When to choose it:

- You need customisation but lack in-house capacity.
- Your requirements are complex or evolving.
- You want to access specialised expertise without long-term hiring.

Pros:

- Flexibility and access to top talent.
- Faster implementation than building alone.
- Lower risk and less overhead than hiring an in-house team.

Cons:

- Ongoing dependency on the partner.
- Need for strong alignment on goals, communication, and IP.
- Potentially higher costs than pure "buy" for complex projects.

Pragmatic Actions:

- Partner Due Diligence: Interview multiple partners, request case studies, and check references to ensure alignment with your sector and goals.
- Define Scope Clearly: Use Statements of Work (SoWs) with milestones, deliverables, and clear exit criteria to avoid scope creep.
- Knowledge Transfer: Build in regular training and documentation sessions so your team can take over routine operations post-project.

- Consulting Model: Consider a "Co-Development Package" where the partner works alongside your team, building internal capability while delivering the solution.
- Regular Reviews: Schedule monthly or quarterly reviews to assess progress, manage risks, and recalibrate objectives as needed.

The Hybrid Approach: Buy-to-Build

Modern AI platforms increasingly allow SMEs to "buy-to-build": start with a robust off-the-shelf solution, then customise features, workflows, or integrations as your needs evolve. This approach balances speed, cost, and flexibility—ideal for SMEs wanting to avoid vendor lock-in or "Frankenstack" risks while still moving quickly.

Decision Framework: How to Choose

Hybrid models are gaining traction among SMEs who want the speed of off-the-shelf solutions but the flexibility to customise as their needs evolve. Platforms like n8n and Zapier exemplify this approach, offering both plug-and-play functionality and extensibility for more advanced use cases.

A structured decision framework helps SMEs avoid costly missteps and ensures technology choices align with business strategy. The right approach is rarely static—business needs, resources, and the tech landscape evolve, so regular reassessment is key.

Ask these questions to guide your decision:

1. How unique are your needs?
    - If highly unique, lean towards building or partnering.
    - If standard, start with 'buy'.

2. How critical is AI to your competitive advantage?
   - If AI is core, invest in building or partnering for differentiation.
   - If it's a support function, buy or buy-to-build.

3. What resources and skills do you have?
   - In-house tech talent? Build or hybrid.
   - Limited tech? Buy or partner.

4. How quickly do you need results?
   - Urgent? Buy or partner.
   - Can you wait? Build or hybrid.

5. What's your risk appetite?
   - Build = higher risk, higher reward.
   - Buy = lower risk, lower reward.
   - Partner = balanced.

6. What's your budget?
   - Building is capital intensive.
   - Buy is OPEX-friendly.
   - Partner can be flexible, but watch for scope creep.

Pragmatic Actions:

- Start Simple: Deploy core features out of the box, then gradually add custom integrations or automations as your team's comfort grows.
- Modular Planning: Choose platforms that support modular add-ons or custom scripting, allowing incremental enhancements.
- Consulting Model: Engage a "Platform Specialist" for a short-term engagement to design and implement custom workflows or integrations, ensuring a smooth transition from standard to tailored solutions.
- Document Customisations: Keep a clear record of all custom features to ease future upgrades or migrations.

More Pragmatic Actions:

- Decision Matrix: Create a simple matrix scoring each option (build, buy, partner, hybrid) against criteria like cost, speed, risk, and fit.
- Scenario Planning: Run "what if" scenarios to test how each approach would perform if your business doubles in size or pivots direction.
- Consulting Model: Use a "Strategy Workshop" facilitated by an independent advisor to guide stakeholders through the decision process and document next steps.
- Review Annually: Revisit your technology choices each year to ensure they still align with your evolving business goals and market conditions.

Tools and Solutions for SMEs

Function	Build (Custom)	Buy (Off-the-Shelf)	Partner/Hybrid
CRM & Sales	In-house dev (rare)	HubSpot, Zoho, Salesforce	Consultancy integration
Marketing Automation	Custom Python/Node	Mailchimp, ActiveCampaign, Jasper	Agency or n8n customization
Operations	Custom workflow apps	QuickBooks, Xero, Zapier, n8n	Systems integrator
HR	Custom portals	BambooHR, Zoho People	HR tech consultants
Analytics	Custom dashboards	Power BI, Tableau, Google Data Studio	Data analytics partner
AI Chatbots	Custom LLM deployment	ChatGPT Plus, Tidio, Drift	AI specialist agency

Note: n8n stands out as a flexible, SME-friendly workflow automation platform that can be bought off-the-shelf, self-hosted (build), or enhanced with partner support for complex integrations.

Practical Tips for SMEs

1. Start with Buy: For most SMEs, buying off-the-shelf tools is the fastest, safest way to deliver early wins and build AI confidence.
2. Partner for Complexity: customise, integrate, or extend your stack—without locking you into expensive custom builds.
3. Build Only When Strategic: Reserve in-house builds for core, differentiated capabilities. Even then, consider hybrid "buy-to-build" models for speed and flexibility.
4. Prioritise Integration: Choose tools with open APIs and strong integration support (e.g., n8n, Zapier, Microsoft Power Automate).
5. Negotiate and Pilot: Always pilot new tools or partnerships before full rollout. Negotiate flexible contracts and clear SLAs.
6. Plan for Change: Technology and business needs evolve—choose solutions and partners that grow with you.

Case Study 1: Micro Business (Under 10 Staff) (illustrative)

Company: "Bright Copy" – B2B Copywriting Agency (8 employees, London)

Challenge:
The founder wanted to automate client proposal creation and email follow-ups but lacked technical expertise and time for custom development.

Approach:
Buy-first strategy.

- Adopted Jasper AI (£39/month) for automated copy generation.
- Used Calendly (free/£8/user/month) for scheduling.

- Integrated with Gmail and Google Drive using Zapier (free/£20/month).

Why Buy?

- Quick deployment (days, not months).
- Minimal setup or technical overhead.
- Vendor support and regular feature updates.

Results:

- Proposal turnaround time halved.
- 10+ admin hours saved per week.
- No need for in-house IT or external consultants.

Lesson:

For most micro businesses, buying off-the-shelf AI tools delivers immediate value with low risk and minimal disruption.

Case Study 2: Medium Enterprise (Under 200 Staff) (illustrative)

Company: "Nova Retail Group" – Specialty Retailer (140 employees, Birmingham)

Challenge:

Nova wanted to unify inventory, sales, and customer data for real-time analytics and predictive stock management. Off-the-shelf tools lacked the integration depth needed, and in-house resources were limited.

Approach:
partnered hybrid strategy.

- Partnered with a local AI consultancy to scope requirements and design a solution.
- Used n8n Pro (€50/month) as the integration backbone, connecting Zoho CRM, QuickBooks, and custom inventory databases.
- The partner built custom n8n workflows and dashboards, then trained Nova's staff for ongoing management.

Why Partner/Hybrid?

- Needed tailored integrations and analytics not available in standard products.
- Avoided the cost and risk of building from scratch.
- Gained access to specialist expertise and ongoing support.

Results:

- Unified data dashboards delivered real-time insights.
- Inventory errors reduced by 60%.
- Staff are empowered to manage and adapt workflows after the initial rollout.

Lesson:
For growing SMEs with more complex needs, partnering with an AI specialist and leveraging flexible platforms like n8n enables rapid, cost-effective innovation without the overhead of a full in-house team.

Conclusion

The "build, buy, or partner" decision is no longer binary for SMEs. The right approach depends on your business goals, resources, and appetite for risk and innovation. For most, the journey begins with buying proven tools, then partnering or building as your needs and ambitions grow. By making smart, pragmatic technology choices—and learning from peers—you can avoid common pitfalls, maximise ROI, and future-proof your business for the AI-powered era.

Key Tools and Platforms for SMEs:

Function	Off-the-Shelf (Buy)	Flexible/Hybrid (Buy-to-Build)	Custom (Build/Partner)
CRM	HubSpot, Zoho	Salesforce + n8n	Custom CRM with partner
Automation	Zapier, Power Automate	n8n Pro/Community	Custom Python/Node scripts
Analytics	Power BI, Tableau	Power BI + n8n	Partner-built dashboards
HR	BambooHR, Zoho People	BambooHR + integration partner	Custom HR portal
AI Chatbots	ChatGPT Plus, Tidio	ChatGPT API + n8n	Bespoke LLM deployment

With this framework, SMEs can confidently navigate the AI technology landscape—delivering smarter, faster, and more cost-effective business growth.

Who can I go to for support that is both cost-effective and will provide clarity around the buy, partner and build options?

AI Support for SME's

Below is a structured overview of where SMEs can find resources and support for each approach:

1. Freelancer & Developer Platforms

These platforms provide access to individual AI developers, data scientists, and project managers on a flexible, project-by-project basis ideal for SMEs wanting to "build" or customise solutions without hiring full-time staff.

Freelancer platforms are a flexible entry point for SMEs that need to "build" or customise AI solutions but lack in-house expertise. These platforms democratise access to global talent, making it possible to find specialists for short-term, project-based, or ongoing support without the overhead of full-time hires. This approach is especially useful for prototyping, automating specific workflows, or bridging temporary skill gaps.

- Upwork: Global marketplace for freelancers in AI, data science, software development, and more.
- Toptal: Curated network of top freelance AI and software professionals.
- Fiverr: Affordable, gig-based access to AI developers, automation experts, and consultants.
- Guru: Connects SMEs with freelance AI and IT professionals for both short- and long-term projects.

Pragmatic Actions:

- Define Your Scope: Before hiring, create a clear project brief outlining deliverables, timeline, and desired outcomes.
- Start Small: Test freelancers with a pilot or limited-scope task to assess quality and fit.

- Leverage Platform Tools: Use built-in vetting, milestone payments, and communication tools to manage risk and ensure accountability.
- Consulting Model: Consider a "Freelancer-as-a-Service" arrangement for ongoing needs, where a small pool of trusted freelancers supports your business on demand.
- Knowledge Transfer: Request documentation and handover sessions to ensure your team can maintain solutions after the project ends.

2. AI Consulting Firms and Agencies

AI consultancies specialise in helping SMEs assess needs, choose tools, develop strategies, and implement solutions whether you want to build, buy, or partner. Many offer workshops, roadmaps, and ongoing support at SME-friendly rates.

AI consultancies offer SMEs access to strategic guidance, technical expertise, and implementation support. They can help you assess readiness, develop a roadmap, and avoid common pitfalls, which is especially valuable for businesses new to AI or facing complex integration challenges. Many consultancies now offer SME-friendly packages, workshops, and flexible engagements.

- help4IT: Offers AI strategy consulting specifically for SMEs, including assessment, roadmap development, and vendor selection. https://help4it.co.uk/
- Ghost Enterprises: Provides AI consulting to improve efficiency and drive innovation, with a focus on practical business outcomes for SMEs. https://ghostenterprises.co.uk/
- Brainpool AI: Delivers custom AI development, machine learning consulting, and tailored solutions for SMEs looking to build or hybridise their approach. https://brainpool.ai/
- Roover: Specialises in AI for mid-market and medium-sized businesses, supporting strategy, implementation, and employee training. https://roover.eu/en/

- TRY AI: UK-based consultancy helping small businesses benefit from AI tools, with hands-on support for tool selection and implementation. https://www.tryai.co.uk/
- RTS Labs: US-based firm with a focus on AI consulting for small businesses, including roadmap creation and change management. https://rtslabs.com/
- RedBlink Technologies: Recognised as a top AI consulting company for small businesses, offering generative AI and automation services. https://redblink.com/
- Cambridge Consultants: Known for advanced AI and machine learning solutions, suitable for SMEs with more complex needs. https://www.cambridgeconsultants.com/

Pragmatic Actions:

- Discovery Workshops: Engage a consultancy for a short "AI Readiness Assessment" or "Strategy Workshop" to clarify goals and identify quick wins.
- Phased Engagement: Structure consulting projects in phases (assessment, pilot, scale-up) with clear deliverables at each stage.
- Request Case Studies: Ask for examples of similar SME projects to gauge experience and fit.
- Ongoing Support: Consider a retainer or "fractional AI officer" model for continuous advice and troubleshooting.
- Internal Capability Building: Include staff training and documentation as part of the consulting engagement to build long-term self-sufficiency.

3. Networks, Accelerators, and Industry Bodies

Industry networks and accelerators provide SMEs with access to expert mentors, peer learning, and sometimes subsidised pilots or grants. These organisations help SMEs benchmark progress, stay updated on best practices, and connect with vetted solution providers.

- Local Chambers of Commerce: Many offer digital transformation programmes, AI workshops, and vendor introductions.
- Digital Catapult (UK): Runs SME-focused AI adoption programmes, readiness assessments, and pilot opportunities.
- Tech Nation (UK/Europe): Provides scale-up support, peer networks, and access to vetted consultants.
- Innovate UK EDGE: Offers innovation and technology advisory for SMEs, including AI partner matching.

Pragmatic Actions:

- Join Local Programs: Participate in digital transformation or AI adoption programmes offered by chambers of commerce or regional accelerators.
- Apply for Subsidised Pilots: Leverage grant programmes or subsidised consulting to offset the cost of experimentation.
- Peer Learning: Attend roundtables and workshops to learn from real-world SME case studies and share your own experiences.
- Consulting Model: Use "Innovation Clinics" or "Peer Advisory Boards" for ongoing support and accountability.

4. Vendor and Platform Support

AI software vendors increasingly recognise SME needs, providing onboarding, training, and integration support as part of their packages. Many also maintain partner directories for more complex deployments or customisations.

If you decide to "buy, "many AI software vendors offer onboarding, training, and integration support—often included in the subscription price or available as add-ons. Some also maintain partner networks of certified consultants.

- HubSpot, Zoho, Salesforce, Microsoft, and Google Cloud all offer SME onboarding, training, and access to certified implementation partners.
- n8n, Zapier, Power Automate: Provide extensive documentation, community forums, and directories of partner agencies for workflow automation and integration.

Pragmatic Actions:

- Onboarding Sessions: Take advantage of free or discounted onboarding and training included with your subscription.
- Pilot First: Test new tools in a sandbox or limited environment before full rollout.
- Integration Support: Ask vendors for access to certified partners if you need help with customisation or complex integrations.
- Community Forums: Use vendor forums and knowledge bases for troubleshooting and best practices.
- Consulting Model: Consider vendor "implementation packages" for rapid deployment and knowledge transfer.

5. Universities and Research Institutes

Many universities run AI innovation labs or offer consulting and student-led projects at reduced rates for SMEs, which can be a cost-effective way to access cutting-edge expertise.

Universities and research institutes can be valuable partners for SMEs seeking affordable, cutting-edge AI expertise. Through innovation labs, student-led projects, and government-backed partnerships, SMEs can access R&D and fresh talent at a fraction of commercial rates; however, any commercial organisation needs to understand the potential different objectives.

- University AI Labs: Look for local or regional university programmes focused on SME engagement.
- Knowledge Transfer Partnerships (UK): Government-backed programmes pairing SMEs with academic experts for AI and digital projects.

Pragmatic Actions:

- Engage with Local Labs: Reach out to university AI labs for collaboration or student project opportunities.
- Apply for KTPs: Use Knowledge Transfer Partnerships or similar programmes to subsidise R&D and access academic expertise.
- Prototype and Validate: Use academic partnerships to prototype new ideas or validate concepts before commercial rollout.
- Internships: Offer student placements for ongoing support and to build a talent pipeline.

6. Peer and Industry Groups

Peer groups and industry forums offer SMEs a trusted environment to share experiences, seek advice, and access sector-specific recommendations. These communities can be invaluable for benchmarking, vendor selection, and troubleshooting.

- LinkedIn Groups, Meetup, and Slack Communities: Join SME AI groups to share experiences, get recommendations, and find collaborators.
- Industry-specific forums: Many sectors (e.g., retail, manufacturing, healthcare) have AI working groups or best-practice networks.

Pragmatic Actions:

- Join Relevant Groups: Participate in LinkedIn, Slack, or Meetup communities focused on AI for your industry.

- Share and Learn: Actively engage in discussions, share your journey, and seek feedback on your AI initiatives.
- Leverage Sector Groups: Use industry-specific forums to access best practices and case studies relevant to your field.
- Consulting Model: Form or join a "Peer Learning Circle" to meet regularly with other SMEs for mutual support and accountability.

Summary Table

Resource Type	Examples/Platforms	Best For (Build, Buy, Partner)
Freelancer Platforms	Upwork, Toptal, Fiverr, Guru	Build, Customization
AI Consulting Firms	help4IT, Ghost Enterprises, Brainpool, Roover, TRY AI, RTS Labs, RedBlink, Cambridge Consultants	Partner, Strategy, Implementation
Networks/Accelerators	Digital Catapult, Tech Nation, Innovate UK EDGE, Chambers of Commerce	Partner, Buy, Pilot Support
Vendor Support	HubSpot, Zoho, Salesforce, n8n, Zapier	Buy, Integration, Training
Universities/Research	University AI Labs, KTPs	Build, Pilot, Cost-effective R&D
Peer Groups	LinkedIn, Meetup, Industry Forums	All (advice, recommendations)

Key Takeaway:

SMEs do not have to navigate the build, buy, or partner decision alone. Whether you need strategic guidance, technical development, or integration support, a growing ecosystem of consultants, agencies, networks, and platforms is available, often with SME-friendly pricing and flexible engagement models. Start with your business objectives, then leverage these resources to make informed, cost-effective AI adoption decisions.

SMEs can accelerate AI adoption and bridge resource gaps by leveraging a broad ecosystem of support, including freelancers, consultancies, networks, vendors, universities, and peer groups. By starting with clear business objectives and using these resources strategically, SMEs can innovate cost-effectively, build internal capability, and remain competitive in a rapidly evolving market.

PART V
SCALING AND OPTIMISATION

CHAPTER 13
Scaling What Works

Moving from Pilot to Production and Expanding Successful AI Initiatives

For small and medium-sized enterprises (SMEs), the journey with AI doesn't end with a successful pilot. In fact, that's just the beginning. The true value of AI is unlocked when businesses move from isolated experiments to integrated, scalable solutions that drive measurable impact across the organisation. This chapter guides you through the practical steps, challenges, and strategies for scaling AI from pilot to production and beyond, supported by real-world case studies and SME-friendly tools.

Why Scaling AI Matters

A successful AI pilot proves potential. But scaling AI and deploying it across more users, processes, or business units delivers the operational efficiency, customer delight, and revenue growth that set market leaders apart. Scaling is about turning "what works" into "what's next", ensuring that AI becomes a sustainable, competitive asset rather than a one-off experiment.

Key benefits of scaling AI for SMEs:

- Efficiency gains: Automate more tasks, freeing up staff for higher-value work.

- Consistent quality: Standardise processes and decision-making across the business.
- Data-driven growth: Leverage insights from larger, more integrated datasets.
- Competitive advantage: Respond faster to market changes and customer needs.

1. Laying the Groundwork: From Pilot to Production

Transitioning from a successful pilot to production is a critical inflection point for SMEs. Many organisations stall at this stage due to underestimating the complexity of scaling—issues like data silos, inconsistent processes, and lack of change management can derail progress. Building a solid foundation ensures that AI initiatives are sustainable and deliver value at scale.

Assess and Document What Worked

Before scaling, rigorously review your pilot:

- Did it meet or exceed your KPIs (cost savings, time reduction, customer satisfaction, etc.)?
- What were the technical and organisational challenges?
- What feedback did users provide?

Document lessons learnt, including data requirements, integration needs, and change management issues. This will help avoid repeating mistakes and ensure smoother scaling.

Build a Scalable Architecture

- Automate data pipelines: Use tools (like Zapier, n8n, or Microsoft Power Automate) to ensure data flows seamlessly between systems.

- Choose scalable platforms: Cloud-based AI tools (Microsoft 365 Copilot, Google Workspace, AWS, etc.) can flex as your needs grow.
- API integration: Ensure your AI models and tools can connect via APIs for easy expansion into new workflows.

Strengthen Data Governance and Quality

Scaling amplifies both good and bad data. Invest in:

- Data cleaning and validation: Automate where possible.
- Clear data ownership: Assign roles and responsibilities.
- Compliance: Ensure GDPR and other data privacy regulations are met.

Upskill and Engage Your Team

- Training: Provide ongoing AI and data literacy training for staff.
- Change management: Communicate the "why" and "how" of scaling AI to build buy-in and reduce resistance.

Pragmatic Actions:

- Conduct a Post-Mortem Workshop: Gather all pilot stakeholders for a structured review session. Use frameworks like "Start, Stop, Continue" to identify what worked, what didn't, and actionable next steps.
- Develop a Scaling Blueprint: Document technical requirements, integration points, and change management lessons in a concise playbook to guide future rollouts.
- Consulting Model: Engage an "AI Scaling Readiness Assessment" with a consultant to audit your architecture, data, and processes, ensuring you're prepared for broader deployment.

- Automate Documentation: Use tools like Notion or Confluence to create living documents that evolve as your AI systems scale.

2. Prioritizing Where to Scale

Not all pilots are equally scalable. SMEs often have limited resources, so it's essential to focus on areas where AI can deliver the most value with the least friction. Prioritisation should be data-driven and aligned with business strategy. Use data and business priorities to identify where AI will have the greatest impact:

- High-volume, repetitive processes: Where automation delivers the biggest time and cost savings (e.g., customer service, invoicing, scheduling).
- Customer-facing functions: Where improved personalisation or responsiveness can boost satisfaction and loyalty.
- Data-rich areas: Where predictive analytics or decision support can drive revenue or efficiency (e.g., sales forecasting, inventory management).

Pragmatic Actions:

- Impact-Effort Matrix: Map potential scaling opportunities on an impact vs effort grid to identify "quick wins" and high-value targets.
- Stakeholder Interviews: Conduct interviews with department heads to surface pain points and assess readiness for AI adoption.
- Consulting Model: Use a "Scaling Opportunity Workshop" facilitated by an external advisor to align leadership on priorities and create a phased rollout plan.
- Pilot Replication: Select adjacent teams or processes similar to your initial pilot for the next phase, minimising customisation and accelerating adoption.

Tip: Start with adjacent processes or departments where the pilot's success can be replicated with minimal customisation.

3. Managing the Transition: From Experiment to Everyday

Scaling AI is as much about people and process as it is about technology. SMEs must address change management, user adoption, and ongoing support to ensure AI becomes part of everyday operations.

Robust Testing and Monitoring

- Test at scale: Pilot with a larger user group or additional departments before full rollout.
- Monitor performance: Use dashboards to track KPIs and flag issues (e.g., model drift, data errors, user adoption).
- Iterate quickly: gather feedback, fix problems, and optimise workflows.

Integration and Automation

- Workflow automation tools: Platforms like n8n (especially for medium enterprises), Zapier, and Microsoft Power Automate are invaluable for orchestrating AI across systems and teams.
- API-first mindset: Ensure new AI tools can integrate easily with your existing tech stack.

Governance and Ethics

- Ethical AI: As you scale, ensure fairness, transparency, and compliance are maintained.
- Auditability: Keep records of AI decisions and data flows for accountability and improvement.

Pragmatic Actions:

- Change Champions: Appoint "AI Ambassadors" in each department to support adoption, gather feedback, and troubleshoot issues.
- Staged Rollouts: Implement AI in waves, starting with the most receptive teams and gradually expanding, using lessons learnt to refine the process.
- Consulting Model: Consider a "Managed AI Rollout" service, where a consultancy oversees deployment, training, and support during the transition.
- Feedback Loops: Establish regular check-ins (e.g., biweekly) for user feedback and rapid iteration.

4. Measuring and Communicating Success

Clear, ongoing measurement is vital to demonstrate value and maintain momentum. Communicating wins and learnings helps sustain buy-in from staff and leadership, while robust metrics guide continuous improvement.

- Business metrics: Track cost savings, revenue growth, customer satisfaction, and employee productivity.
- Technical metrics: Monitor model accuracy, uptime, and response times.
- User adoption: Measure engagement, satisfaction, and feedback from staff and customers.
- Continuous improvement: Use insights from scaled deployments to refine models, processes, and training.

Pragmatic Actions:

- Real-Time Dashboards: Deploy business intelligence tools (e.g., Power BI, Tableau, Google Data Studio) to visualise key metrics and share progress transparently.

- Success Stories: Document and share case studies internally, highlighting tangible benefits and user testimonials.
- Consulting Model: Engage a "Value Realisation Consultant" to help quantify ROI, refine KPIs, and develop communication materials for stakeholders.
- Recognition Programs: Celebrate teams or individuals who contribute to successful scaling, reinforcing positive behaviours and engagement.

Practical Steps for Scaling AI in SMEs

1. Document and Analyze Pilot Success: Capture workflows, data needs, and lessons learnt. Identify what made the pilot work and what needs adjustment.
2. Prioritise Scaling Opportunities: Focus on processes with high impact and minimal customisation needs. Use data to guide decisions.
3. Invest in Scalable Tools and Integration: Choose cloud-based, API-friendly platforms. Use workflow automation (n8n, Zapier, Power Automate) to connect systems.
4. Strengthen Data Foundations: Ensure data quality, governance, and compliance are robust enough to support larger-scale AI.
5. Upskill and Engage Your Team: Provide training, communicate benefits, and involve staff in scaling efforts. Offer ongoing training and microlearning modules to keep staff AI-literate as systems evolve.
6. Monitor, Measure, and Iterate: Use dashboards and KPIs to track progress. Gather feedback and optimise continuously.
7. Maintain Governance and Ethics: Scale responsibly, with clear policies for data privacy, fairness, and transparency.
8. Iterative Governance: Update data governance and ethical guidelines as AI scales, ensuring compliance and trust keep pace with expansion.

9. Peer Learning: Join SME AI user groups or industry forums to exchange scaling strategies and avoid common pitfalls.
10. Annual Review: Schedule an annual "AI Health Check" with an external advisor to reassess architecture, processes, and business alignment as your AI footprint grows.

Case Study 1: Micro Business (Under 10 Staff) (illustrative)

Company: "EcoGlow Candles" – Artisan Candle Maker (7 employees, Bristol)

Pilot:
Automated customer email responses and order tracking using ChatGPT Plus (£16/month) and Zapier (free tier).

Scaling Up:
After seeing a 50% drop in customer response times and a 20% increase in repeat orders, EcoGlow expanded automation to:

- Social media DMs and Facebook Messenger using ManyChat (free/£15/month).
- Inventory updates and supplier notifications via Zapier integrations.
- Personalised marketing emails using Jasper AI (£39/month).

How They Did It:

- Documented pilot workflows and success metrics.
- Used Zapier to connect new channels and automate repetitive tasks.
- Trained all staff on using and monitoring AI tools.
- Set up monthly reviews to refine automations and address issues.

Results (12 months):

- Customer response time cut by 65%.
- Admin time reduced by 10+ hours/week.

- Sales are up 18% year over year.
- No additional hires are needed despite business growth.

Takeaway:
A clear, incremental scaling plan allowed EcoGlow to extend AI benefits across the business, driving efficiency and customer delight with minimal extra cost.

Case Study 2: Medium Enterprise (Under 200 Staff) (illustrative)

Company: "Nova Retail Group" – Specialty Retailer (140 employees, Birmingham)

Pilot:
Implemented predictive inventory management using Microsoft 365 Copilot (£24/user/month) and n8n Pro (€50/month) to automate data flows between sales, inventory, and suppliers.

Scaling Up:
With a 15% reduction in stockouts and £40,000 saved in inventory costs, Nova expanded AI to:

- Dynamic pricing and personalised promotions using Salesforce Einstein (SME pricing).
- Automated sales forecasting and replenishment workflows across all store locations.
- Integrated customer feedback analysis using Sprout Social (£79/month) and n8n for sentiment-driven marketing adjustments.

How They Did It:

- Standardised data formats and governance across departments.

- Used n8n as the central automation hub, connecting CRM, ERP, and marketing tools.
- Provided AI and data training for store managers and key staff.
- Established a cross-functional AI steering group to oversee scaling and continuous improvement.

Results (18 months):

- Inventory holding costs are down 22%.
- Revenue per customer is up 19%.
- Customer satisfaction scores improved by 25%.
- AI-driven processes now support 80% of routine operational decisions.

Takeaway:
By investing in scalable architecture, robust governance, and staff upskilling, Nova Retail Group turned a single AI pilot into a company-wide transformation delivering measurable business value and future-proofing their operations.

Conclusion

Scaling AI is the difference between isolated innovation and transformative business change. For SMEs, the path from pilot to production is achievable with the right blend of practical tools, robust data, and empowered people. Start with what works, scale thoughtfully, and let AI become a core driver of your business's growth and resilience.

Key Tools for Scaling AI in SMEs:

Function	Free Option	Paid Option (Best Value)
Automation	Zapier Free	n8n Pro (€50/mo, ~£43/mo)
Customer Service	Tidio Free	ChatGPT Plus (£16/mo)
Inventory/Finance	Google Sheets	Microsoft 365 Copilot (£24/user/mo)
Marketing	Mailchimp Free	Jasper AI (£39/mo), Sprout Social (£79/mo)
Analytics	Google Data Studio	Salesforce Einstein (SME pricing)

With these strategies and tools, SMEs can confidently move from successful pilots to scaled, sustainable AI adoption—unlocking new levels of efficiency, customer value, and growth.

CHAPTER 14

Managing AI Risks, Ethics, and Compliance - Don't Skip This One!

Privacy, Security, Bias, Ethical, and Regulatory Considerations Made Simple

Artificial Intelligence (AI) is revolutionising how small and medium-sized enterprises (SMEs) operate, unlocking efficiencies, automating routine tasks, and providing powerful insights. Yet, as AI becomes more central to business operations, so too does the need to manage its risks. For SMEs, the stakes are high: privacy breaches, biased algorithms, and regulatory missteps can erode customer trust, lead to legal trouble, and damage hard-earned reputations. As AI becomes embedded in everyday business operations, SMEs face increasing scrutiny from customers, regulators, and partners regarding how they use and manage AI. The introduction of new regulations such as the EU AI Act, alongside growing public concern over privacy and bias, means that even smaller businesses cannot afford to overlook these issues. Proactively managing risks and compliance not only protects against legal and reputational harm but can also build customer trust and differentiate your business in the market. The good news? With the right approach, managing AI risks, ethics, and compliance can be straightforward, affordable, and even a source of competitive advantage.

1. Privacy: Protecting Data in an AI World

Data privacy is a top concern as SMEs collect and process more customer and employee information through AI systems. Regulatory requirements (GDPR, CCPA, EU AI Act) are becoming stricter, with significant penalties for non-compliance even for small businesses.

Risks:

- Unauthorized access to customer or employee data
- Inadvertent sharing of sensitive information
- Non-compliance with GDPR, CCPA, or sector-specific rules

SME Solutions:

- Data minimisation: Only collect and retain what you truly need.
- Encryption and access controls: Use built-in security tools in cloud platforms (e.g., Microsoft 365, Google Workspace).
- Regular audits: Schedule quarterly reviews to check where sensitive data is stored and who has access.
- Privacy-focused AI tools: For example, Nightfall AI (from $99/month) scans cloud apps for sensitive data leaks.

Pragmatic Actions:

- Data Mapping: Create a visual map of all data flows in your business, identifying where sensitive data is collected, stored, and processed.
- Privacy Impact Assessments: Conduct regular privacy impact assessments for new AI projects to identify and mitigate risks early.
- Consulting Model: Engage a privacy consultant for a "Data Protection Health Check", a short-term review of your current practices with actionable recommendations.
- Staff Awareness: Run annual privacy training sessions for all employees, using real-world SME scenarios.

Action:
Document your data flows, restrict access to sensitive data, and use privacy-by-design principles in all new AI projects.

2. Security: Safeguarding AI Systems

AI introduces new security risks, including attacks on models, data poisoning, and vulnerabilities in third-party tools. SMEs are increasingly targeted due to perceived weaker defences.

Risks:

- Cyberattacks targeting AI models or training data
- Vulnerabilities in third-party AI tools
- Weaknesses in integration points (e.g., APIs)

SME Solutions:

- Secure integration: Use workflow automation platforms like Zapier or n8n to connect tools without exposing sensitive APIs.
- Threat detection: Tools like Microsoft Defender (included in 365 subscriptions) and Darktrace (SME pricing) monitor for unusual activity.
- Vendor vetting: Choose AI tools with clear, transparent security practices and certifications (e.g., SOC 2).

Pragmatic Actions:

- Security by Design: Integrate security reviews into every stage of your AI project lifecycle, from procurement to deployment.
- Penetration Testing: Schedule annual penetration tests that include AI systems and integrations.
- Consulting Model: Use a "Virtual CISO" (Chief Information Security Officer) service for periodic security audits and incident response planning tailored to SMEs.

- Incident Response Plan: Develop and rehearse a simple incident response plan covering AI-specific risks.

Action:
Include AI systems in your regular cybersecurity reviews and penetration testing.

3. Bias: Ensuring Fair and Ethical Outcomes

AI systems can unintentionally perpetuate or amplify bias, especially if training data is incomplete or unrepresentative. This can lead to unfair outcomes and regulatory scrutiny, particularly in sensitive areas like hiring, lending, or customer service.

Risks:

- Discriminatory outcomes in hiring, lending, or customer service
- Training data that reflects or amplifies historical biases

SME Solutions:

- Bias detection: Use open-source tools like Fairlearn or IBM AI Fairness 360 to regularly assess your AI models.
- Diverse data: Audit your training datasets for representation gaps using tools like DiversifyAI.
- Human oversight: Always keep a human in the loop for critical decisions, especially in hiring, lending, or customer-facing roles.

Pragmatic Actions:

- Bias Audits: Schedule quarterly bias audits using open-source tools and document findings and mitigation steps.
- Diverse Data Sourcing: Proactively seek diverse data sources and involve a cross-section of staff in reviewing training data for gaps.

- Consulting Model: Engage an AI ethics consultant for a "Bias Mitigation Workshop" to build internal capability and establish best practices.
- Transparency Reports: Publish simple, plain-language reports on how your business addresses AI bias.

Action:
Document your efforts to identify and mitigate bias, and be transparent about how AI is used in your business.

4. Ethics: Building Trust Through Transparency

Public trust in AI depends on transparency and responsible use. SMEs can gain a competitive edge by demonstrating ethical leadership, clearly explaining how AI is used and ensuring it aligns with company values.

Risks:

- Lack of transparency in AI-driven decisions
- Misuse of AI-generated content (e.g., deepfakes, plagiarism)

SME Solutions:

- Explainability: Use tools like LIME or SHAP to help explain AI model predictions in plain language.
- Transparency: Clearly disclose to customers and staff when AI is being used (e.g., "This chatbot is powered by AI").
- Content checks: Use Grammarly or Copyleaks to check for plagiarism or inappropriate content in AI-generated text.

Pragmatic Actions:

- AI Ethics Policy: Develop and publish a concise AI ethics policy, co-created with input from staff and stakeholders.

- Explainability Tools: Use tools like LIME or SHAP to generate understandable explanations for AI-driven decisions, and share these with affected users.
- Consulting Model: Consider a "Responsible AI" workshop series facilitated by an external expert to help define and embed ethical principles.
- Customer Communication: Clearly label AI-powered interactions and provide channels for feedback or concerns.

Action:
Publish a simple AI ethics policy and make it accessible to customers and employees.

5. Compliance: Navigating Regulations

The regulatory landscape for AI is evolving rapidly, with new rules such as the EU AI Act introducing specific obligations for SMEs. Staying compliant is not just about avoiding fines; it's about future-proofing your business and maintaining access to markets.

Risks:

- Fines for violating GDPR, the EU AI Act, or industry-specific rules
- Difficulty keeping up with evolving regulations

SME Solutions:

- Compliance automation: Tools like Alyne (SME pricing) or SeamlessAI (from $99/month) help track regulatory changes and automate compliance tasks.
- Templates and sandboxes: Use free templates from the EU AI Act and participate in regulatory sandboxes to test high-risk AI systems.
- Assign responsibility: Even a part-time compliance officer can make a big difference.

Pragmatic Actions:

- Compliance Calendar: Maintain a compliance calendar with key regulatory deadlines, review dates, and training refreshers.
- Regulatory Sandboxes Participate in regulatory sandboxes to test new AI solutions under real-world conditions with guidance from authorities.
- Consulting Model: Use a compliance consultant for a "Regulatory Gap Analysis" to identify and address weaknesses before they become liabilities.
- Documentation: Keep clear, organised records of all compliance activities and decisions for audit readiness.

Action:
Keep clear records of your compliance efforts and update policies as regulations evolve.

How Can SMEs Stay Up-to-Date with AI Risks, Ethics and Regulations

AI risks, ethics, and regulations are moving targets. SMEs that make continuous learning and engagement part of their culture are better equipped to adapt and thrive.

SMEs can stay up to date on AI risks, ethics, and compliance by leveraging a mix of regulatory resources, targeted training, industry events, and practical tools designed specifically for their needs. The evolving regulatory landscape, especially with the introduction of the EU AI Act, means that proactive, ongoing education and engagement are essential for both compliance and competitive advantage.

1. Engage with Regulatory Guidance and Support

- EU AI Act SME Provisions: The EU AI Act specifically addresses SMEs by offering simplified documentation, reduced compliance fees, and proportional obligations. SMEs are given priority access to regulatory sandboxes, which allow them to test AI systems in real-world conditions with regulatory oversight and minimal administrative burden. These sandboxes and dedicated SME support channels provide up-to-date guidance, best practices, and answers to compliance questions.
- National and EU Communication Channels: Many Member States have established dedicated service desks or hotlines for SMEs, such as the Austrian Service Desk for AI, to help navigate compliance and implementation questions.

2. Participate in Industry Events and Webinars

- Digital SME Alliance & Sector Bodies: Organisations like the European DIGITAL SME Alliance regularly host webinars, panel discussions, and workshops focused on AI Act compliance, risk management, and best practices for SMEs. These events feature expert panels, Q&A sessions, and presentations of new compliance tools, offering practical, up-to-date advice.
- Institute of Directors (IoD): Events like "Generative AI Governance: a guide for UK SMEs" provide actionable governance insights and networking opportunities for business leaders.

3. Invest in AI Literacy and Staff Training

- AI Literacy Programs: The EU and national bodies support AI literacy through training courses specifically tailored to SMEs. These programmes cover responsible AI use, risk management, and

regulatory requirements, ensuring that both leaders and staff understand the latest developments and compliance obligations.
- Online Training Platforms: Providers such as Coursera, K.I.T.A., and Skillcast offer flexible, up-to-date courses on AI ethics, risk, and compliance, enabling SMEs to upskill at their own pace.
- Vendor Training: Many AI vendors (Microsoft, Google, etc.) offer compliance and security training as part of their onboarding for SME clients.

4. Leverage Practical Compliance Tools

- Conformity Assessment Tools: The European DIGITAL SME Alliance and others have developed online tools to help SMEs assess their AI systems for compliance with the AI Act and other regulations.
- Automated Monitoring: Security and compliance platforms (e.g., Nightfall AI, Alyne, Microsoft Defender) provide ongoing monitoring for privacy, security, and bias risks, alerting SMEs to new threats or compliance gaps as they arise.

5. Monitor Trusted Information Sources

- Regulatory Websites: Regularly check the European Commission's AI Act portal and national data protection authorities for updates, guidance, and new requirements.
- Industry Newsletters and Blogs: Subscribe to reputable sources such as NAVEX, Cyber Insights, and sector-specific compliance blogs for the latest developments, case studies, and practical tips.

6. Join Peer Networks and Forums

- Professional Networks: Engage with LinkedIn groups, Slack communities, and local business forums focused on AI, compliance, and digital transformation. Peer sharing is a powerful way to learn about new risks, solutions, and regulatory changes.
- Standardisation and Advisory Forums: SMEs are encouraged to participate in standard-setting and advisory forums under the AI Act, ensuring their perspectives are represented and that they receive early notice of regulatory changes.

7. Adopt a Continuous Learning and Review Culture

- Regular Internal Reviews: Schedule periodic reviews of your AI systems, data practices, and compliance policies to ensure they remain current as regulations and technologies evolve.
- Update Policies and Training: Revise internal policies and staff training materials as new

Pragmatic Actions:

- Industry Engagement: Assign a staff member to monitor regulatory updates and participate in relevant webinars, forums, and industry groups.
- Quarterly Policy Reviews: Schedule quarterly internal reviews to update policies, procedures, and training based on new risks or regulatory changes.
- Peer Learning: Join SME-focused AI networks or advisory boards to share experiences and learn from others' compliance journeys.
- Consulting Model: Consider an annual "AI Risk & Compliance Health Check" with an external advisor to benchmark progress and identify emerging issues.

Case Study 1: Micro Business (Under 10 Staff) (illustrative)

Company: "ContentCraft" – Copywriting Agency (6 employees, Edinburgh)

Challenge:
ContentCraft began using ChatGPT to draft client content. Clients raised questions about originality, and the founder worried about potential privacy breaches and bias in generated text.

Actions Taken:

- Plagiarism and content checks: Subscribed to Copyleaks ($10.99/month) to scan all AI-generated drafts before delivery.
- Transparency: Added clear disclaimers to contracts and email footers, explaining when AI was used in content creation.
- Bias review: Periodically used Fairlearn to check for gender or cultural bias in generated content.
- Data security: Restricted access to client files, used encrypted cloud storage (Google Workspace), and regularly reviewed permissions.

Results:

- No plagiarism incidents in over 500 client projects.
- Positive client feedback on transparency and ethical standards.
- Improved trust, leading to a 20% increase in repeat business.

Lesson:
With basic tools and clear communication, even the smallest businesses can manage AI risks and build customer trust without heavy investment.

Case Study 2: Medium Enterprise (Under 200 Staff) (illustrative)

Company: "Rubix" – Manufacturing SME (UK, 120 employees)

- **Challenge: compliance.** Rubix deployed an AI-powered predictive maintenance system to monitor machinery. The system collected sensitive operational data and made automated decisions about equipment servicing, raising concerns about data privacy, security, and regulatory compliance.

Actions Taken:

- Data governance: Implemented strict access controls and encrypted all sensor data stored in the cloud.
- Vendor due diligence: Choose an AI provider with SOC 2 certification and transparent security documentation.
- Bias and fairness: Used IBM AI Fairness 360 to ensure maintenance decisions did not inadvertently favour certain machines or shift patterns, preventing operational bias.
- Compliance: Appointed a part-time compliance lead to oversee GDPR adherence and maintain documentation for the EU AI Act.
- Explainability: Used LIME (Local Interpretable Model/Agnostic Explanations; this is a common data science tool) to generate easy-to-understand explanations for maintenance decisions, which were shared with staff and auditors.

Results:

- Achieved a 40% reduction in unplanned downtime, with no reported data breaches or compliance issues.
- Passed an external audit with commendations for transparency and data management.
- Staff reported increased trust in the AI system, improving adoption and collaboration.

Lesson:

A proactive, structured approach to AI risk and compliance enabled Rubix to scale its AI initiative confidently, unlocking operational value while safeguarding ethics and trust.

Summary Table: Staying Up to Date

Method	Example Resources/Actions
Regulatory Guidance	EU AI Act SME portal, national AI service desks
Industry Events & Webinars	Digital SME Alliance, IoD, sector webinars
AI Literacy & Training	Coursera, K.I.T.A, Skillcast, vendor training
Compliance Tools	Digital SME Alliance conformity tools, Nightfall AI, Alyne
News & Updates	NAVEX, Cyber Insights, regulatory newsletters
Peer Networks	LinkedIn groups, Slack, local business forums
Standardization & Advisory Forums	AI Act advisory forums, standardization bodies
Continuous Review	Scheduled audits, policy updates, staff refreshers

In summary:

SMEs should combine regulatory resources, targeted training, industry engagement, and practical compliance tools to stay current on AI risks, ethics, and compliance. Provisions in the EU AI Act and national initiatives make it easier than ever for SMEs to access support, training, and up-to-date information tailored to their needs. By embedding continuous learning and review into their culture, SMEs can confidently manage AI risks and turn responsible AI adoption into a competitive advantage.

Conclusion: Turning Compliance into Competitive Advantage

Managing AI risks, ethics, and compliance is not just about avoiding problems—it's about building a resilient, trustworthy business. For SMEs, the path is clear:

- Start simple: Use affordable, off-the-shelf tools to address privacy, security, and bias.
- Be transparent: Clearly communicate how and why you use AI.
- Stay proactive: regularly review, audit, and update your policies as technology and regulations evolve.
- Empower your team: Provide basic training on AI ethics and compliance.

By embedding ethical and compliant AI practices into your operations, you not only protect your business—you build trust with customers, partners, and regulators, turning risk management into a source of competitive strength.

Essential Tools for SME AI Risk Management:

Function	Free Option	Paid Option (Best Value)
Privacy	Google Workspace	Nightfall AI ($99/mo)
Security	Microsoft Defender	Darktrace (SME pricing)
Bias Detection	Fairlearn, IBM AIF360	DiversifyAI (trial)
Explainability	LIME, SHAP	N/A (open source)
Compliance	Templates (EU AI Act)	Alyne, SeamlessAI ($99/mo)
Content Checks	Grammarly Free	Copyleaks ($10.99/mo)

With these practices and tools, SMEs can confidently harness AI's power—responsibly, ethically, and in full compliance with today's evolving standards.

CHAPTER 15

Building an AI-Ready Culture

Change Management, Training, and Creating Organisational Buy-In

Artificial intelligence is not just a technological upgrade; it is a cultural transformation. For small and medium-sized enterprises (SMEs), the difference between AI success and stagnation often comes down to people, not algorithms. Building an AI-ready culture means fostering openness to change, investing in practical training, and creating genuine organisational buy-in at every level. This chapter offers a pragmatic roadmap, grounded in research and real SME experience, to help you lead your team through the journey of AI adoption.

1. Why Culture Matters in AI Adoption

AI's true value is unlocked when it becomes part of how your business thinks and operates. 70% of digital transformations fail due to cultural resistance, not technical limitations. For SMEs, where teams often wear multiple hats, fostering an AI-ready culture is critical to ensuring tools are adopted, trusted, and used effectively. A culture of continuous learning and psychological safety empowers employees to experiment, fail, and iterate – key for maximising AI's potential. Research shows that top-management involvement and a culture of continuous learning are fundamental for successful AI implementation in SMEs. Change management is not a one-off event but a process of renewing direction, structure, and capabilities to meet evolving needs.

Key drivers of successful AI culture:

- Leadership commitment: Senior management must champion AI, communicate its value, and model openness to change.
- Clear communication: Explaining the "why" behind AI reduces fear and resistance.
- Employee empowerment: Involving staff in the process builds trust and surfaces practical insights.
- Continuous learning: Ongoing training and feedback loops foster confidence and competence.
- Ethical alignment: Addressing ethical concerns and job impacts with empathy builds credibility and trust.

Pragmatic Actions:

- Conduct a "Cultural Readiness Audit": Use surveys or focus groups to assess current attitudes toward AI, identifying fears (e.g., job displacement) and knowledge gaps.
- Leadership Immersion: Require senior leaders to complete hands-on AI training (e.g., using ChatGPT for strategy drafting) and share their learnings company-wide.
- Consulting Model: Engage a "Culture Transformation Advisor" for a 6-week sprint to co-design values, rituals, and communication plans aligned with AI goals.

2. Change Management: Turning Resistance into Resilience

SMEs often lack formal change management frameworks, leading to fragmented AI adoption. Structured approaches like the ADKAR model (Awareness, Desire, Knowledge, Ability, Reinforcement) can help SMEs navigate resistance and build momentum incrementally. Change management is the structured approach that helps organisations adapt to new technologies like AI. For SMEs, this means:

- Mapping the journey: Use cognitive mapping or collaborative workshops to identify concerns, opportunities, and key initiatives.
- Anticipating resistance: Use surveys or AI-powered sentiment analysis to surface anxieties early.
- Personalising communication: Tailor messages to different teams and roles, addressing specific worries and benefits.
- Celebrating quick wins: Share early successes to build momentum and reinforce positive attitudes.

Pragmatic Actions:

- ADKAR Workshops: Run workshops to map each team's journey through the ADKAR stages, addressing blockers at each phase.
- AI Impact Mapping: Collaboratively diagram how AI will affect workflows, roles, and decision-making to preempt concerns.
- Consulting Model: Hire a fractional change manager to design and execute a 90-day AI adoption plan, including stakeholder analysis and resistance mitigation strategies.
- Feedback Loops: Implement biweekly "AI Pulse Checks" using tools like Microsoft Forms to monitor sentiment and adjust tactics.

Best practice:
Beyond tools like AKDAR (Awareness, Desire, Knowledge, Ability and Reinforcement), leverage the McKinsey 7S Model or similar frameworks to align strategy, structure, systems, shared values, skills, style, and staff with your AI vision.

3. Training: Building Confidence and Competence

Only 34% of SMEs provide AI training, yet 89% of employees report anxiety about using AI tools. Role-specific, bite-sized learning increases adoption by 50% compared to generic courses. It will cost significantly more to hire "AI ready" staff than to train your existing talent. AI adoption is less about coding and more about digital literacy, critical thinking, and collaboration. Effective training for SMEs includes:

- Role-based learning: Focus on practical skills relevant to each job function (e.g., using AI in marketing, HR, or operations).
- Blended formats: Combine online micro-courses (Coursera, LinkedIn Learning), vendor-led workshops, and peer learning sessions.
- Continuous refreshers: Offer regular updates as AI tools and business needs evolve.
- On-demand support: Use AI-powered chatbots or knowledge bases to answer staff questions in real time.

Pragmatic Actions:

- Microlearning Modules: Develop 5–10 minute video tutorials (using tools like Loom) focused on specific AI tasks (e.g., "Using ChatGPT for Customer Service Scripts").
- Peer Mentorship: Pair AI-hesitant staff with "AI Champions" for weekly 30-minute skill-sharing sessions.
- Consulting Model: Partner with a training provider for a "Learn-as-You-Build" programme, where staff develop AI solutions (e.g., a chatbot) while mastering tools.
- Gamification: Create friendly competitions (e.g., "AI Hackathons") with rewards for the most creative automation or efficiency gains, suitable for medium-sized organisations and very effective.

Affordable tools:

- Coursera, FutureLearn, LinkedIn Learning: AI literacy and digital skills courses (free to £30/month).
- Vorecol HRMS, Leena AI: AI-driven onboarding and training modules (SME pricing).
- Internal champions: Identify tech-savvy staff to act as "AI buddies" or local trainers.

Practical Steps for Building an AI-Ready Culture

1. Secure leadership commitment: Ensure top management actively supports and models AI adoption.
2. Map the change journey: Use collaborative workshops or cognitive mapping to surface concerns and opportunities.
3. Invest in practical, ongoing training: make learning accessible, relevant, and continuous.
4. Foster open communication: address fears, celebrate wins, and share progress regularly.
5. Empower local champions: Identify and support early adopters to drive peer learning.
6. Embed ethics and inclusion: Make responsible AI use a visible, ongoing conversation.
7. Iterate and adapt: Use feedback and analytics to refine your approach and sustain momentum.

4. Creating Organisational Buy-In

Employees are 3x more likely to support AI initiatives if they contribute ideas during planning. SMEs benefit from democratising the AI journey, turning sceptics into co-creators. Buy-in is not achieved through mandates but through shared ownership and visible value. To foster buy-in:

- Involve staff early: Invite feedback on AI tool selection and pilot design.
- Be transparent: Clearly communicate AI's purpose, benefits, and limitations.
- Address job concerns: Acknowledge fears about automation and focus on how AI augments, not replaces, human roles.
- Measure and share impact: Regularly report on time saved, errors reduced, or customer satisfaction improved.
- Reward participation: recognise and celebrate employees who champion AI or suggest improvements.

Pragmatic Actions:

- Co-Design Sprints: Host cross-functional workshops where employees brainstorm AI use cases for their workflows. Prototype top ideas in real time.
- Transparency Boards: Use physical or digital boards to track AI projects, including goals, progress, and challenges.
- Consulting Model: Engage a "Participatory Design Facilitator" to run ideation sessions and build consensus on AI priorities.
- Job Redesign Workshops: Help teams reimagine roles with AI, focusing on upskilling opportunities (e.g., shifting from data entry to data analysis).

5. Sustaining the Change: Embedding AI in Everyday Work

Without deliberate reinforcement, 60% of AI initiatives lose momentum within a year. SMEs must embed AI into daily rituals, metrics, and leadership behaviours to sustain change.

- Iterative improvement: Use feedback loops and AI-driven analytics to refine processes and training.

- Cultural rituals: Make AI part of team meetings, performance reviews, and strategy sessions.
- Ethical leadership: Maintain open discussions about AI ethics, privacy, and fairness as part of your culture.
- Leadership modelling: Senior leaders should use AI tools themselves and share their experiences.

Pragmatic Actions:

- AI-Driven Performance Reviews: Include AI literacy and tool adoption as 10–15% of annual performance goals.
- Monthly "AI Showcases": Dedicate 30 minutes in all-hands meetings to demo new AI workflows and celebrate team successes.
- Consulting Model: Retain a "Culture Sustainment Coach" for quarterly check-ins to refresh training, address fatigue, and align AI use with evolving goals.
- Ethics Roundtables: Host quarterly discussions on AI risks (bias, privacy) to maintain trust and accountability.

Cross-Cutting Strategy: The AI Playbook

- Create a Living Document: Develop a simple, shared AI playbook outlining tools, best practices, and success stories. Update it monthly with employee contributions.
- Leverage SME Agility: Use your smaller size to pilot cultural experiments (e.g., "AI Fridays" for exploration) and scale what works quickly.

By integrating these additions, SMEs can transform AI adoption from a technical project into a cultural advantage driving innovation, retention, and growth.

Case Study 1: Micro Business (Under 10 Staff) (illustrative)

Company: "Fresh Grounds" – Independent Coffee Shop (6 employees, Glasgow)

Challenge:
Staff were anxious about a new AI-powered scheduling and inventory system, fearing job loss and increased surveillance.

Approach:

- Leadership commitment: The owner led by example, learning the system first and sharing her own learning curve.
- Collaborative mapping: Used a whiteboard session (inspired by cognitive mapping) to list staff concerns and potential benefits.
- Role-based training: Provided hands-on demos tailored to each role (barista, manager, supplier liaison).
- Transparency: Explained that AI would automate only repetitive admin, freeing staff for customer engagement and creativity.
- Quick wins: Celebrated when the AI system reduced shift conflicts and stockouts, sharing results in team meetings.

Results:

- Staff reported higher job satisfaction and less stress about scheduling.
- Inventory errors dropped by 40%, and customer service ratings improved.
- Employees began suggesting new ways to use AI, such as for customer loyalty programmes.

Lesson:
Small teams benefit from open dialogue, visible leadership, and practical, role-specific training.

Case Study 2: Medium Enterprise (Under 200 Staff) (illustrative)

Company: "Nova Retail Group" – Specialty Retailer (140 employees, Birmingham)

Challenge:
Rolling out AI-powered sales forecasting and automated customer support across multiple locations met resistance from both frontline staff and middle managers.

Approach:

- Top-down and bottom-up engagement: Senior leaders communicated the strategic vision, while local managers held listening sessions to gather concerns and ideas.
- AI champions: Identified early adopters in each department to act as "AI buddies", supporting peers and feeding back issues.
- Blended training: Used LinkedIn Learning for digital skills, vendor-led workshops for tool-specific training, and peer-led lunch-and-learns.
- Transparent metrics: Shared dashboards showing improvements in sales accuracy, customer response times, and workload reduction.
- Ethics and inclusion: Hosted open forums to discuss AI ethics, privacy, and the future of work, reassuring staff about upskilling and redeployment opportunities.

Results:

- AI adoption rates exceeded 85% within six months.
- Sales forecast accuracy improved by 20%, and customer support satisfaction rose by 25%.
- Staff turnover dropped, and employee engagement scores increased.

Lesson:

A structured, inclusive approach combining leadership vision, local champions, and transparent communication drives sustainable buy-in and cultural change at scale.

Conclusion

Building an AI-ready culture is not about technology alone; it's about people, purpose, and participation. For SMEs, success comes from strong leadership, open communication, practical training, and a relentless focus on shared value. By making change management, learning, and buy-in central to your AI journey, you can unlock not just smarter processes, but a more engaged, innovative, and resilient organisation.

Key Tools and Solutions for Culture Change in SMEs:

Function	Free Option	Paid Option (Best Value)
Training	Coursera, LinkedIn	Vorecol HRMS, Leena AI (SME)
Communication	Slack, Teams, Miro	Microsoft 365, Google Workspace
Change Management	Whiteboards, Miro	Vorecol HRMS, Monday.com
Feedback/Surveys	Google Forms	CultureAmp, Officevibe
AI Champions	Internal volunteers	Peer incentives, small rewards

With these strategies and tools, any SME can foster a culture that not only accepts AI but thrives on it—turning change into a catalyst for growth and lasting success.

PART VI
LOOKING FORWARD

CHAPTER 16
Measuring AI ROI

Tracking business impact and justifying continued investment objectives.

By rigorously measuring ROI, SMEs can avoid wasted spend, secure stakeholder buy-in, and confidently scale what works. Moreover, clear ROI measurement helps SMEs prioritise high-impact projects, justify further investment, and build a data-driven culture that supports continuous improvement.

Artificial Intelligence (AI) promises transformative benefits for small and medium-sized enterprises (SMEs) — from cost savings and efficiency gains to revenue growth and improved customer experience. This chapter offers a clear, actionable framework for tracking AI business impact, justifying continued investment, and building a data-driven case for scaling AI across your organisation.

Why Measuring AI ROI Matters

Measuring ROI is not just about financial reporting; it's about ensuring AI projects align with your business goals, deliver real value, and inform smarter decisions about where to invest next. According to PwC, businesses that measure ROI on their AI projects are 1.7 times more likely to achieve their AI goals. For SMEs, demonstrating ROI is essential for securing buy-in, managing risk, and scaling what works.

The Fundamentals: How to Measure AI ROI

8. Define Clear Objectives and Metrics

Setting specific, business-aligned objectives is the foundation for meaningful ROI measurement. Objectives should go beyond generic goals and be tailored to your unique pain points, such as reducing late payments, boosting online sales, or improving customer response times.

Start by identifying what success looks like for your AI project. Common objectives include:

- Cost savings: reduced labour, fewer errors, lower operational costs.
- Revenue growth: increased sales, higher conversion rates, improved customer retention.
- Efficiency gains: time saved, faster processes, increased productivity.
- Customer satisfaction: Higher CSAT scores, faster response times, better reviews.

Pragmatic Actions:

- Stakeholder Workshop: Hold a workshop with key staff to define what "success" looks like for your AI project, ensuring alignment with business strategy.
- Consulting Model: Engage an AI advisor for a "KPI Mapping Session" to translate business goals into measurable AI metrics. OKRs (Objectives and Key Results) is another term tool to monitor your progress with a more granular approach and shorter timescale cycles and a personal favourite.

- SMART Metrics: Use the SMART (Specific, Measurable, Achievable, Relevant, Time-bound) framework to set clear targets for each metric (e.g., "Reduce manual scheduling time by 75% within 3 months").

2. Establish Baseline Performance

Without a clear "before" picture, it's impossible to prove the impact of AI. Baselines create the reference point for all future comparisons and are essential for isolating AI-driven improvements. Before implementing AI, gather baseline data on your key metrics (e.g., monthly labour hours, average handle time, sales conversion rates, customer satisfaction scores). This enables you to make apples-to-apples comparisons post-implementation.

Pragmatic Actions:

- Data Audit: Collect historical data on all relevant KPIs (e.g., labour hours, error rates, sales conversion) prior to AI implementation.
- Baseline Dashboard: Set up a simple dashboard in Excel or Google Sheets to visualise pre-AI performance.
- Consulting Model: Use a "Baseline Assessment Package" from a consultant to ensure your data is clean, consistent, and ready for comparison.

9. Calculate Total Costs

Many SMEs underestimate the true cost of AI by omitting integration, training, or ongoing support (sometimes true of larger companies as well!). A comprehensive cost analysis ensures ROI calculations are accurate and credible. Credible.

Include all costs:

- Software subscriptions and licenses

- Setup and integration
- Training and onboarding
- Ongoing support and maintenance

Typical SME AI costs range from £500–£20,000+ for setup, and £100–£5,000+ per month for ongoing expenses.

Pragmatic Actions:

- Cost Tracking Template: Create a template to log all direct and indirect costs software, hardware, integration, training, support, and staff time.
- Scenario Planning: Estimate costs for best-case and worst-case scenarios to understand potential ROI ranges.
- Consulting Model: Engage a financial analyst or AI consultant for a "Total Cost of Ownership (TCO) Review" to avoid hidden expenses.

10. Track and Quantify Benefits

AI benefits often extend beyond immediate cost savings—think improved cash flow, higher customer retention, or faster delivery times. Quantifying both tangible and intangible benefits provides a holistic view of ROI.

Monitor changes in your KPIs after deploying AI. For example:

- Hours saved per week/month
- Reduction in error rates or late payments
- Increase in average order value or customer retention

Pragmatic Actions:

- Monthly Impact Reviews: Schedule regular reviews to track changes in KPIs post-AI deployment.

- Case Study Documentation: Document real-world examples (e.g., "AI-powered invoicing reduced late payments by 20% and saved £2,400 annually"1).
- Consulting Model: Use a "benefit realisation workshop" to identify and quantify both financial and non-financial gains.

11. Calculate ROI

The standard ROI formula (Net Gain from Investment / Investment Cost) × 100 remains the gold standard for financial justification. However, SMEs should also consider "time to value" and break-even analysis to set realistic expectations.

Basic ROI Formula

ROI (%) = [(Total Benefits − Total Costs) ÷ Total Costs] × 100

Detailed 3-Year ROI Calculation

Total Investment Cost Formula:

Total Investment = Initial Investment + (Annual Ongoing Costs × Number of Years)

Where:

Initial Investment = Software + Implementation + Training + Consulting + Hardware

Annual Ongoing Costs = Licensing + Maintenance + Additional Training

Total Benefits Formula:

Annual Benefits = Cost Savings + Revenue Increases

Cost Savings = Labour Savings + Operational Savings + Error Reduction Savings

Revenue Increases = (Current Revenue × Efficiency Gain %) + New Revenue Streams

Net Present Value (NPV) Formula:

NPV = Σ [Cash Flow Year n ÷ (1 + Discount Rate)^n] − Initial Investment

Where:

Cash Flow Year n = Annual Benefits − Annual Ongoing Costs

Discount Rate = Typically 8-12% for SMEs

n = Year number (1, 2, 3…)

Payback Period Formula:

Simple Payback Period = Initial Investment ÷ Annual Net Cash Flow

Where:

Annual Net Cash Flow = Annual Benefits − Annual Ongoing Costs

Internal Rate of Return (IRR) Formula:

0 = Σ [Cash Flow Year n ÷ (1 + IRR)^n] − Initial Investment

(Solved iteratively or using financial calculator/software)

Component Calculations

Labour Cost Savings:

Annual Labour Savings = (Hours Saved per Week × 52 weeks × Hourly Rate × Number of Staff)

Example:

(10 hours × 52 × £25 × 3 staff) = £39,000 annually

Revenue Increase:

Revenue Increase = Current Annual Revenue × Improvement Percentage

Example:

£500,000 × 15% = £75,000 additional revenue

Total Cost of Ownership (TCO):

3-Year TCO = Initial Investment + (Annual Costs × 3) + (One-off Costs)

Complete 3-Year ROI Formula:

3-Year ROI (%) = [(((Annual Benefits × 3) − (Initial Investment + (Annual Costs × 3)))
÷ (Initial Investment + (Annual Costs × 3))] × 100

Worked Example Using a Realistic Scenario:

Initial Investment = £75,000
Annual Ongoing Costs = £35,000
Annual Benefits = £125,000

Total Investment = £75,000 + (£35,000 × 3) = £180,000
Total Benefits = £125,000 × 3 = £375,000
Net Profit = £375,000 - £180,000 = £195,000
ROI = (£195,000 ÷ £180,000) × 100 = 108.33%

Monthly Cash Flow Formula:

Monthly Net Cash Flow = (Annual Benefits – Annual Ongoing Costs) ÷ 12

Payback Period (months) = Initial Investment ÷ Monthly Net Cash Flow

Risk-Adjusted ROI Formula:

Risk-Adjusted ROI = Standard ROI × (1 – Risk Factor) Risk Factor = Where Risk 0.15 to 0.30 (15-30% reduction for implementation risks)

These formulas provide the mathematical foundation for calculating AI implementation ROI and can be easily implemented in spreadsheets or financial planning tools.

Pragmatic Actions:

- ROI Calculator: Build a simple calculator in Excel or Google Sheets to automate ROI computations for each project.
- Break-Even Analysis: Determine how many months it will take for AI benefits to outweigh costs, and communicate this timeline to stakeholders.
- Consulting Model: Leverage an external advisor for an "ROI Validation Review" to ensure your calculations are robust and credible.

12. Find the Break-Even Point

Knowing when your investment will start to pay off is crucial for planning and stakeholder confidence. The break-even point helps SMEs manage cash flow and set realistic targets for future AI investments. Determine how long it will take for the benefits to outweigh the costs. This helps set realistic expectations and guides future investment decisions.

Pragmatic Actions:

- Visual Timeline: Create a visual break-even chart to show when cumulative benefits surpass total costs.
- Scenario Testing: Model different adoption rates or benefit levels to see how they affect your break-even timeline.
- Consulting Model: Use a "Financial Milestone Planning" session with your accountant or consultant to integrate AI ROI into your broader business planning.

13. Measuring Intangible and Long-Term Benefits

AI can deliver softer benefits like improved employee morale, better decision-making, or enhanced brand reputation that are harder to quantify but still significant.

Pragmatic Actions:

- Qualitative Surveys: Use staff and customer surveys to capture changes in satisfaction, confidence, or perceived value.
- Storytelling: Collect anecdotes and testimonials to supplement quantitative ROI data and support broader buy-in.
- Consulting Model: Hire a communications consultant for a "Value Storytelling Workshop" to help articulate and share these intangible gains.

Pragmatic Actions:

- Quarterly ROI Reviews: Schedule quarterly check-ins to reassess costs, benefits, and KPIs.
- Iterative Scaling: Use ROI data to prioritise which AI projects to expand or replicate across the business.
- Peer Benchmarking: Compare your results with industry peers to identify areas for improvement or new best practices.

14. Continuous Improvement and Scaling

ROI measurement is not a one-time task. Regularly reviewing and refining your approach ensures ongoing value and helps identify new opportunities for AI investment.

Key Metrics for AI ROI in SMEs

- Financial: Cost reductions, revenue growth, improved cash flow
- Operational: Faster task completion, fewer errors, higher productivity
- Customer Experience: Improved satisfaction and retention rates
- Time to Value: How quickly the benefits are realized after implementation

Tools and Solutions for Measuring AI ROI

- Dialzara: AI-powered virtual receptionist and call handling (from $49/month)
- HubSpot CRM: AI-driven sales and marketing automation (free/paid)
- QuickBooks AI: Automated invoicing and financial analytics (from $12/month)

- Zapier/n8n: Workflow automation and integration (free/paid)
- Google Sheets/Excel: For tracking and visualizing ROI metrics (free/low cost)
- Customer satisfaction tools: SurveyMonkey, Google Forms, or built-in CSAT features in CRM platforms

Best Practices for Tracking and Justifying AI ROI

1. Start with a Pilot: Focus on a single use case with clear, measurable outcomes.
2. Track Baseline and Ongoing Metrics: Use before-and-after comparisons to isolate AI impact.
3. Include All Costs: Don't forget setup, training, and ongoing support.
4. Measure Both Tangible and Intangible Benefits: Include cost savings, revenue, efficiency, and customer satisfaction.
5. Communicate Results: Share ROI data with leadership and staff to build buy-in for future AI investments.
6. Review and Reinvest: Regularly review performance and reallocate resources to the highest-ROI projects.

Case Study 1: Green Thumb Landscaping (Under 10 Staff) (illustrative)

Industry: Landscaping Services
Location: USA
Company Size: 15 employees
Source: [Dialzara]

Challenge:
Green Thumb Landscaping spent excessive time on manual scheduling and invoicing. The owner handled all scheduling, which took 4 hours per week, and invoicing was slow, with frequent late payments.

AI Solutions Implemented

- AI-powered scheduling assistant: Cloud-based app with AI features ($100/month subscription)
- Automated invoicing system: AI-driven platform ($50/month subscription)

ROI Calculation

Scheduling:

- Time spent dropped from 4 hours to 1 hour per week
- Savings: About $900 in labor costs over 6 months

Invoicing:

- Invoicing time reduced from 6 to 2 hours monthly
- Late payments dropped from 30% to 10%
- Savings: $720 in labor costs over 12 months, plus $2,400 annually from improved cash flow

Total 12-Month ROI:

- Total Costs: $1,800 (subscriptions and staff time)
- Total Benefits: $4,020 (labor savings and cash flow improvements)
- ROI: (($4,020 − $1,800) / $1,800) × 100 = 123%

Key Takeaways

- Small businesses can realise significant ROI from affordable, off-the-shelf AI tools.
- Focused automation of repetitive tasks frees up time for growth and customer service.

- Tracking labour savings and cash flow improvements provides a clear business case for continued AI investment.

Case Study 2: Tech Training Incubator (Under 200 Staff) (illustrative)

Industry: Education/Training
Location: USA
Company Size: ~100 employees
Source: [Dialzara]

Challenge

The incubator struggled to respond rapidly to student enquiries. Response times averaged 24 hours, and staff spent significant time answering repetitive questions.

AI Solutions Implemented

- AI-powered customer service chatbot: Automated responses to common student enquiries, handling over 80% of questions.

ROI Calculation

- Response time reduced: From 24 hours to 6 hours
- Annual labor savings: $120,000 (from reduced staff time and improved efficiency)
- Improved student satisfaction: Faster answers led to higher retention and positive feedback

ROI Formula Used:

ROI = Net Benefits / Total Costs × 100

$$ROI = \frac{\text{Net Benefits}}{\text{Total Costs}} \times 100$$

Assuming annual AI costs (software, setup, training) of $40,000:
ROI=120,000−40,00040,000×100=200%

$$ROI = \frac{120,000 - 40,000}{40,000} \times 100 = 200\%$$

Key Takeaways

- AI-driven customer service delivers rapid, measurable efficiency gains for medium-sized organisations.
- ROI is not just about cost savings—improved satisfaction and retention are equally important.
- Calculating ROI based on labour savings and customer metrics provides a strong case for further AI adoption.

Additional Real-World Example: E-Commerce AI Recommendations

A small e-commerce business implemented an AI-powered recommendation engine to personalise product suggestions.

- KPIs Tracked: Conversion rate, average order value, and customer lifetime value

- Outcome: ROI of 250% in the first year, as incremental revenue far outweighed software and training costs.

Conclusion

For SMEs, measuring AI ROI is critical to ensuring investments deliver real business value. By starting small, tracking the right metrics, and using clear ROI calculations, you can justify continued investment, scale successful initiatives, and build a data-driven culture of innovation. With affordable tools and a disciplined approach, even the smallest business can unlock the full potential of AI, turning insight into impact and experimentation into sustainable growth.

CHAPTER 17

Future-Proofing Your Business

Staying Ahead of AI Trends and Maintaining Competitive Advantage

AI is no longer a distant promise for small and medium-sized enterprises (SMEs); it's an everyday business tool, rapidly evolving and reshaping how companies operate, compete, and grow. The businesses that thrive will be those that don't just adopt AI but build a culture and strategy to keep pace with its relentless innovation. This chapter offers a practical roadmap for future-proofing your SME, with actionable advice, real-world case studies, and a focus on affordable, accessible solutions.

1. The New AI Imperative for SMEs

AI adoption among SMEs has accelerated dramatically. In 2025, two-thirds of small business owners report that AI has already had a significant impact on their business, and more than three-quarters expect this impact to grow in the next two years. AI is no longer a buzzword; it's central to productivity, decision-making, and customer engagement. AI's integration into core business processes has shifted from a competitive advantage to a basic requirement for survival. The rapid democratisation of AI driven by cloud platforms, open-source tools, and SME-focused solutions means that even the smallest businesses can now access capabilities once reserved for large enterprises. However, this accessibility also raises the bar: customers, partners, and regulators expect SMEs to leverage AI ethically and effectively. Future-proofing is not just about technology but about building organisational agility, resilience, and a proactive approach to change.

Why future-proofing matters:

- Competition: AI levels the playing field, enabling SMEs to compete with much larger rivals.
- Customer expectations: personalised, instant, and seamless experiences are now the norm, driven by AI-powered tools.
- Pace of change: AI tools, platforms, and best practices are evolving rapidly. Businesses that lag risk being left behind.

Pragmatic Actions:

- Leadership Briefings: Schedule quarterly leadership sessions to review AI trends and assess strategic implications for your business.
- Consulting Model: Engage an "AI Foresight Advisor" for an annual review of your AI maturity and to co-create a future-proofing roadmap tailored to your sector.
- Customer Listening: Use AI-powered sentiment analysis tools to monitor changing customer expectations and adapt offerings accordingly.

2. Key AI Trends Shaping SME Success in 2025 and Beyond

a. AI as a Core Business Tool

The AI landscape is evolving at breakneck speed, with new capabilities emerging every quarter. SMEs that stay alert to these trends, such as agentic AI, unified communications, and accessible design tools, can pivot faster and capture new opportunities ahead of competitors. Continuous learning and adaptation are now essential elements of business strategy. AI is already embedded in everyday business operations, from chatbots and intelligent search to automated scheduling and marketing. Tools like Microsoft 365 Copilot, ChatGPT, and Zoho CRM's Zia AI are becoming standard for SMEs seeking efficiency and insight.

b. Agentic and Autonomous AI

The next wave is "agentic AI", autonomous agents that can plan, learn, and take action across business functions with minimal human intervention. Solutions like Salesforce Agentforce and managed AI services are making this accessible to SMEs, not just large enterprises. This is an important technology with many organisations like GitHub and n8n providing pre-built agentic solutions integrating common technologies. The agent is like a worker who manages tasks in a process.

c. Unified Communication and Collaboration

AI-powered platforms (e.g., Zoom AI Companion, Dropbox Dash) streamline communication, automate note-taking, and provide advanced search across all business content, reducing wasted time and boosting productivity.

d. Personalized, Integrated Marketing

AI-driven marketing platforms now offer seamless integration across social, email, and web, enabling SMEs to deliver hyper-personalised campaigns and recommendations at scale.

e. Accessible AI for Design and Content

Affordable tools like Canva (with AI-powered design features) and Grammarly are democratising professional content creation for SMEs, regardless of in-house expertise.

f. Continuous Learning and Skills Development

The rapid evolution of AI means continuous upskilling is essential. SMEs are leveraging online bootcamps, vendor-led training, and peer networks to stay current. It costs far less to upskill your own staff than hire in an "AI ready" member of staff; invest in your people, and it will pay dividends in motivation and commitment supporting that all-important cultural journey.

Pragmatic Actions:

- Trend Scanning: Assign a team member as your "AI Scout" to track new tools, platforms, and case studies, reporting monthly on relevant developments.
- Peer Benchmarking: Join SME AI user groups or industry roundtables to exchange insights on emerging trends and adoption challenges.
- Consulting Model: Use an "AI Trend Workshop" facilitated by an external expert to educate staff and leadership on the latest developments and their practical implications.

3. Strategies for Staying Ahead

a. Adopt a Continuous Innovation Mindset

- Make experimentation with new AI tools a regular part of your business.
- Encourage staff to test, review, and recommend emerging solutions.
- Innovation Sprints: Run quarterly "AI Innovation Days" where staff experiment with new tools and pitch ideas for process improvements.
- Failure-Friendly Culture: Celebrate lessons learnt from unsuccessful pilots to encourage experimentation and reduce fear of failure.

b. Build Strong Vendor Partnerships

- Choose vendors with clear AI roadmaps and a track record of regular updates.
- Stay engaged with vendor communities and user groups for early access to new features.
- Vendor Scorecards: Develop a scorecard to evaluate vendors on their AI roadmap, support quality, and pace of innovation.
- User Group Participation: Actively participate in vendor user groups to gain early access to beta features and influence product direction.

c. Invest in Data Foundations

- Ensure your data is clean, integrated, and accessible—this is the fuel for current and future AI tools.
- Use tools like Zoho CRM, Microsoft 365, or Dropbox Dash to centralise and manage business information.
- Data Health Audits: Schedule annual data audits to ensure information is clean, integrated, and ready for new AI tools.
- Consulting Model: Hire a data governance consultant for a "Data Readiness Assessment" to identify gaps and recommend improvements.

d. Prioritize AI Literacy and Training

- Regularly invest in staff training through online courses, webinars, and workshops.
- Leverage free resources like the business connected hub for digital and AI upskilling.
- Personalised Learning Paths: Tailor AI training to different roles, focusing on practical applications relevant to each department.
- Microlearning: Offer short, frequent learning modules to keep skills current as tools evolve.

e. Monitor and Benchmark

- Track key metrics (productivity, customer satisfaction, revenue growth) to measure AI impact and identify new opportunities.
- Benchmark against industry peers to spot gaps and areas for improvement.
- KPI (Key Performance Indicators) & OKR (Objectives and Key Results) Dashboards: Implement real-time dashboards to track AI impact on productivity, sales, and customer satisfaction.
- Industry Benchmarks: Subscribe to industry benchmarking reports to compare your progress and spot emerging best practices.

f. Embrace Responsible AI

- Stay informed about AI ethics, data privacy, and compliance requirements.
- Use AI responsibly to build trust with customers, partners, and regulators.
- Ethics Committees: Establish a small internal or cross-functional ethics group to review AI projects and ensure alignment with company values.
- Compliance Updates: Assign responsibility for monitoring new AI regulations and updating practices as needed.

4. Tools and Solutions for Future-Proofing (2025)

The proliferation of SME-friendly AI tools means that future-proofing is more about selecting, integrating, and iterating than about building from scratch. The right mix of free and paid solutions can deliver enterprise-grade capabilities at a fraction of the historical cost.

Pragmatic Actions:

- Tool Pilots: Pilot at least one new AI tool per quarter, documenting results and lessons learnt for broader rollout.
- Integration Playbooks: Develop simple playbooks for integrating new tools into your existing workflows, with clear steps and troubleshooting tips.
- Consulting Model: Use a "Tool Selection Sprint" with an external advisor to shortlist and test solutions that align with your business needs and budget.

Function	Free/Low-Cost Option	Paid/Enterprise Option
Productivity/Automation	Microsoft 365 Copilot (trial)	Microsoft 365 Copilot (£24/user/mo)
Communication	Zoom AI Companion (included)	Zoom AI Suite (SMB pricing)
Design & Content	Canva Free, Grammarly Free	Canva Pro (£10.99/mo)
CRM/Customer Insights	Zoho CRM Free	Zoho CRM Zia AI (£20+/mo)
Marketing Automation	Mailchimp Free, Buffer Free	Salesforce Starter, HubSpot
File Management	Dropbox Dash for Business	Dropbox Advanced
AI Chatbot	ChatGPT Free	ChatGPT Plus (£16/mo)

Practical Steps to Future-Proof Your SME

Future-proofing is an ongoing process, not a one-off project. The most successful SMEs embed regular review, experimentation, and upskilling into their business rhythms.

- Annual AI Strategy Review: Set a recurring date to review your AI strategy, update your roadmap, and reallocate resources based on results and new opportunities.
- Cross-Functional AI Teams: Form small, agile teams from different departments to champion AI adoption and share best practices.
- Continuous Feedback Loops: Use AI-powered analytics to gather real-time feedback on tool effectiveness and staff adoption, iterating quickly as needs change.
- Consulting Model: Engage a "Continuous Innovation Partner" for quarterly check-ins, trend briefings, and on-demand support as your business and the AI landscape evolve.
- Audit your current AI usage: Identify gaps and opportunities across all business functions.
- Stay plugged into trends: follow industry news, attend webinars, and join peer networks to keep up with the latest tools and best practices.
- Pilot new tools regularly: Dedicate time each quarter to trial and review emerging AI solutions.
- Invest in your people: make AI literacy and digital skills a core part of your staff development plan.
- Monitor vendor roadmaps: Choose partners committed to innovation and regular updates.
- Benchmark and measure: Track key metrics and compare against industry peers to ensure you're not falling behind.
- Plan for responsible AI: Build ethics, privacy, and compliance into every AI project.

Case Study 1: Micro Business (Under 10 Staff) (illustrative)

Company: The Social Bean Café (8 employees, UK)

Challenge:

Faced with rising competition and limited marketing resources, The Social Bean Café needed to boost customer engagement and streamline daily operations without hiring more staff.

AI Solutions Adopted:

- ChatGPT (OpenAI): Automated responses to customer enquiries on social media and email, reducing response time from hours to minutes.
- Canva AI: Enabled staff to quickly create professional marketing visuals and social posts without a designer.
- Dropbox Dash: Unified search and content management, allowing the team to find files, recipes, and supplier contracts instantly.

Results:

- 40% increase in customer engagement on social channels.
- 15% rise in repeat business, attributed to faster, more personalised communications.
- Staff saved an average of 5 hours per week on admin and content creation, freeing time for customer service and innovation.

Lessons for SMEs:

- Affordable, off-the-shelf AI tools can deliver rapid, measurable impact even for the smallest teams.
- Unified content management and automation are key to reclaiming time for high-value work.

Case Study 2: Medium Enterprise (Under 200 Staff) (illustrative)

Company: GreenTech Distributors (120 employees, UK)

Challenge:

As a fast-growing supplier of eco-friendly products, GreenTech needed to scale its sales and marketing, improve forecasting, and maintain a personal touch with customers, all while keeping costs in check.

AI Solutions Adopted:

- Microsoft 365 Copilot: Automated meeting notes, document summaries, and advanced search across all business data, boosting team productivity.
- Zoho CRM Zia AI: AI-driven sales forecasting, lead scoring, and customer insights enabled smarter targeting and improved conversion rates.
- Salesforce Agentforce: Piloted autonomous AI agents for routine sales follow-up and customer onboarding, freeing sales staff to focus on complex deals.
- Grammarly: Ensured all customer communications were clear, consistent, and professional.

Results:

- Sales conversion rates increased by 20% within six months.
- Forecasting accuracy improved, reducing overstock and missed sales opportunities.
- Customer satisfaction scores rose by 18% due to faster, more tailored responses.
- The business was able to scale without a proportional increase in headcount.

Lessons for SMEs:

- Integrating AI across sales, marketing, and operations creates compounding benefits.
- Piloting agentic AI solutions prepares SMEs for the next evolution in business automation.
- Continuous upskilling and vendor engagement are essential to maintain momentum.

Conclusion

Staying ahead in the AI era is not about chasing every new trend—it's about building an adaptable, learning-focused business that can absorb change and turn it into a competitive advantage. SMEs that combine the right tools, strong vendor relationships, continuous learning, and a commitment to responsible AI will not only survive but thrive in a rapidly evolving landscape.

Whether you're a team of eight or 180, the future belongs to those who are ready to experiment, learn, and lead with AI.

CHAPTER 18

The AI Horizon for SMEs

Navigating the Next Three Years and beyond

Over the next three years (2025–2027), artificial intelligence will cease to be an optional upgrade for small and medium-sized enterprises (SMEs) and become as fundamental as electricity or broadband. The pace of change isn't slowing—it's accelerating, with AI evolving from a productivity booster to a core driver of growth, efficiency, and competitive differentiation. For SMEs, this isn't about chasing futuristic trends; it's about pragmatic adaptation to survive and thrive. Here's what you need to watch, why it matters, and how to turn these shifts into tangible business growth.

Key Areas to Watch

1. AI Agents Take the Wheel
   - What's changing: "Agentic AI"—autonomous systems that plan, learn, and act with minimal human input—will move from theory to practice. Think of tools like Salesforce Agentforce or bespoke SME solutions handling tasks end-to-end: negotiating supplier contracts, managing inventory, or even drafting marketing campaigns.
   - Impact: These agents will slash operational costs (up to 90% for routine tasks) and free your team for high-value work. But they'll

also demand robust oversight to avoid costly errors or ethical missteps.
- o Growth lever: Start piloting agentic tools in contained areas like customer service or invoicing. Measure time saved and reinvest it into innovation.

2. Hyper-Personalisation Becomes Standard
   - o What's changing: AI won't just recommend products; it'll predict customer needs before they arise. Retailers will see 25% higher order values via AI-driven personalisation, while B2B firms use it to tailor proposals dynamically.
   - o Impact: Customers now expect this level of service. SMEs that deliver it will outpace competitors; those that don't risk irrelevance.
   - o Growth lever: Use affordable tools like Zoho CRM's Zia AI or HubSpot to analyse customer data. Start small—segment one customer group and personalise their journey—then scale.

3. Industry-Specific AI Solutions Proliferate
   - o What's changing: Off-the-shelf AI is giving way to niche solutions for sectors like retail, manufacturing, or professional services. Examples include AI stock management for shops or compliance bots for accountancy firms.
   - o Impact: These tools will democratise capabilities once reserved for large corporations. A local bakery could use AI to optimise supply chains as effectively as a multinational.
   - o Growth lever: Audit your sector's AI landscape annually. Join industry forums or work with consultants to identify tools that solve *your* unique pain points.

4. Ethical AI Becomes a Brand Imperative
   - o What's changing: Regulations (like the EU AI Act) and consumer scrutiny will force SMEs to prioritise fairness, transparency, and

data privacy. Expect stricter rules around AI-driven hiring or customer profiling.
- o   Impact: Trust is now a competitive asset. SMEs that ethically deploy AI will build loyal customers; those that cut corners face reputational damage and fines.
- o   Growth lever: Appoint an internal "AI ethics champion" and conduct quarterly bias audits. Document your compliance—it's a marketing advantage.

5. Skills Shift from Technical to Strategic
   - o   What's changing: As AI handles more execution, SME teams will focus on interpreting insights, managing AI systems, and innovating. Upskilling won't be optional—it'll be survival.
   - o   Impact: A skills gap could leave SMEs behind. Those that invest in AI literacy will see faster adoption and higher ROI.
   - o   Growth lever: Partner with local universities for low-cost training or use microlearning platforms like LinkedIn Learning. Foster a culture where staff experiment with AI weekly.

The Business Impacts: Opportunities and Pitfalls

- Opportunities:
  - o   Efficiency at scale: AI will automate 40–50% of administrative tasks by 2027, letting SMEs operate like larger firms without the overhead.
  - o   Data as a differentiator: SMEs with clean, integrated data will unlock predictive insights (e.g., forecasting cash flow dips) faster than slower-moving rivals.
  - o   Global reach: AI-powered translation and localisation tools will help SMEs enter new markets with minimal risk.

- Pitfalls to Avoid:
  - Tool overload: Don't chase every new AI platform. Focus on 1–2 solutions that align with core business goals.
  - Underestimating data governance: AI is only as good as your data. Start auditing data quality *now* to avoid costly rework later.
  - Neglecting the human element: AI can't replace leadership. Ensure decisions involving ethics or strategy remain human-led.

How SMEs Can Leverage These Changes

1. Start with a "Tomorrow Audit"
   - Every quarter, review: *What repetitive tasks drain our time? Where do competitors use AI better?* Use free frameworks like SWOT to prioritise AI projects.

2. Embrace the Hybrid Approach
   - Blend off-the-shelf tools (e.g., ChatGPT for content) with customisable platforms like n8n for workflow automation. This balances cost and control.

3. Build Partnerships
   - Collaborate with AI consultancies (e.g., TRY AI or Brainpool) for "AI Sprint" projects—fixed-fee, short-term pilots that de-risk experimentation.

4. Measure What Matters
   - Track not just cost savings, but *strategic* metrics:
     - Customer retention (Did personalisation boost loyalty?).
     - Innovation rate (How many ideas came from AI insights?).
     - Employee satisfaction (Has AI reduced burnout?).

5. Future-Proof Your Culture
   - Run monthly "AI Showcases" where staff demo new tools. Reward innovation—even failed experiments offer lessons.

The Bottom Line

The next three years will separate SMEs that view AI as a tactical tool from those weaving it into their strategic DNA. The winners won't be the biggest or wealthiest—they'll be the most adaptable. By focusing on ethical, industry-specific AI and empowering your people to harness it, you'll do more than survive the shift. You'll redefine what your business can achieve.

Action takeaway:
This week, pick one area where AI could save 5 hours of labour. Pilot a tool, measure the impact, and share the results with your team. Momentum starts small—but it compounds fast.

Printed in Dunstable, United Kingdom

64507054R00137